The New York Times

PUBLIC PROFILES
Serena Williams

THE NEW YORK TIMES EDITORIAL STAFF

Published in 2019 by The New York Times® Educational Publishing
in association with The Rosen Publishing Group, Inc.
29 East 21st Street, New York, NY 10010

Contains material from The New York Times® and is reprinted by permission. Copyright © 2019 The New York Times. All rights reserved.

Rosen Publishing materials copyright © 2019 The Rosen Publishing Group, Inc. All rights reserved. Distributed exclusively by Rosen Publishing.

First Edition

The New York Times
Alex Ward: Editorial Director, Book Development
Phyllis Collazo: Photo Rights/Permissions Editor
Heidi Giovine: Administrative Manager

Rosen Publishing
Megan Kellerman: Managing Editor
Erica Grove: Editor
Greg Tucker: Creative Director
Brian Garvey: Art Director

Cataloging-in-Publication Data
Names: New York Times Company.
Title: Serena Williams / edited by the New York Times editorial staff.
Description: New York : New York Times Educational Publishing, 2019. | Series: Public profiles | Includes glossary and index.
Identifiers: ISBN 9781642821758 (library bound) | ISBN 9781642821741 (pbk.) | ISBN 9781642821765 (ebook)
Subjects: LCSH: Williams, Serena, 1981—Juvenile literature. | Tennis players—United States—Juvenile literature. | African American women tennis players—Juvenile literature.
Classification: LCC GV994.W55 S474 2019 | DDC 796.342092—dc23

Manufactured in the United States of America

On the cover: Serena Williams in action against Simona Halep of Romania in the Women's Singles Quarterfinal match on day 10 of the 2016 U.S. Open Tennis Tournament; Tim Clayton/Corbis Sport/Getty Images.

Contents

8   Introduction

CHAPTER 1

Early Career and Stardom

11   Teen-Ager, Fighting to Turn Pro at 14, Puts Off Lawsuit for Now
BY ROBIN FINN

13   A Family Tradition at Age 14 **BY ROBIN FINN**

17   By Knocking Spirlea Out, Serena Williams May Get to Face Her Sister Next **BY ROBIN FINN**

20   Serena Williams Leaves Her Mark on Davenport **BY ROBIN FINN**

22   Serena Williams Will Put Streak on Line Against Hingis
BY ROBIN FINN

25   It's 3 Sets and Pout for Serena Williams **BY ROBIN FINN**

28   U. S. Open; Serena Williams Wins Match, Then Takes a Shot at Hingis **BY SELENA ROBERTS**

31   U.S. Open; Serena Williams Sizes Up Seles, and Wins
BY ROBIN FINN

35   U.S. Open; Little Sister Becomes the Stardust Half **BY ROBIN FINN**

39   Failing to Find Rhythm, Serena Williams Ousted
BY CHRISTOPHER CLAREY

42 Sydney 2000: Tennis; Who Could Ask for Anything More?
BY SELENA ROBERTS

45 Serena Williams Wins As the Boos Pour Down BY SELENA ROBERTS

49 Sports of The Times; Center Stage for Families and Dramas
BY HARVEY ARATON

CHAPTER 2

Mid-Career Trials and Triumphs

52 Serena Williams Needs Some of Agassi's Grit BY SELENA ROBERTS

56 Williams Could Use an Etiquette Lesson BY SELENA ROBERTS

59 Serena Williams Isn't Able to Defend Her Title
BY CHRISTOPHER CLAREY

63 Making Tennis the Top Priority Brings Serena Williams the No. 1 Ranking BY KATIE THOMAS

65 Returning to the Top, but With a New View BY BEN ROTHENBERG

CHAPTER 3

Professional Maturity and Competing as a Mother

68 Surprising Even Herself, Williams Rallies to Title
BY CHRISTOPHER CLAREY

73 Dominant in Her Era, Serena Still Has Time to Build on Legacy
BY CHRISTOPHER CLAREY

77 Serena Williams Will Soon Be 35. But Will She Ever Be No. 1 Again? BY CHRISTOPHER CLAREY

82 Winning While Pregnant: How Athletes Do It BY RONI CARYN RABIN

86 After 'a Lot of Ups and Downs,' Serena Williams Nears Her Return BY CHRISTOPHER CLAREY

90 Tennis Needs Serena Williams Back. But Does She Need to Be Seeded? BY CHRISTOPHER CLAREY

95 The 'Real Serena' Emerges and Roars Back at the French Open
BY CHRISTOPHER CLAREY

99 Serena Williams and Maria Sharapova to Reboot a Rivalry After Life Intervened BY CHRISTOPHER CLAREY

103 No Storybook Ending for Serena Williams. Instead, a Wimbledon Title for Angelique Kerber. BY CHRISTOPHER CLAREY

CHAPTER 4

Venus and Serena: Teammates, Rivals and Sisters

108 In Williams vs. Williams, Big Sister Moves Ahead BY ROBIN FINN

111 Another Sister Showdown for Williamses BY CHRISTOPHER CLAREY

113 Continents Apart, Williams Sisters Make History BY SAL A. ZANCA

117 Playing in Draw's Opposite Sides Benefits the Williamses and the Game BY ROBIN FINN

120 U.S. Open; Unstoppable Team Williams Takes Doubles Title
BY ROBIN FINN

122 Williams Sisters Learned to Think Off Court, Too BY SELENA ROBERTS

126 The Williamses, Reluctant Rivals, Will Battle for the French Title
BY SELENA ROBERTS

129 Williamses' Rivalry Is Close and Compelling, if Not Classic
BY CHRISTOPHER CLAREY

133 A Final Match for Venus and Serena Williams. But Maybe Not the Last One. **BY CHRISTOPHER CLAREY**

138 Grand Sibling Rivalry Leaves Venus Williams a Distinct Underdog **BY VICTOR MATHER AND NAILA-JEAN MEYERS**

143 In Serena Williams's Comeback, a Familiar Opponent: Venus **BY CHRISTOPHER CLAREY**

147 On the Doubles Court, Venus and Serena Williams Make Time Stand Still **BY CHRISTOPHER CLAREY**

150 For Serena Williams, a Memorable U.S. Open Final for the Wrong Reasons **BY BEN ROTHENBERG**

CHAPTER 5

Life in the Spotlight and Advocacy

155 The Tennis Balls Were White Once, Too **BY LIZ ROBBINS**

158 Noticed; Williamsmania Sweeps The Black A-List **BY LIZ ROBBINS**

161 They're Young. They're Sexy. They're Targets. **BY SELENA ROBERTS**

165 Williamses Aren't Outsiders, But They're Still Different **BY SELENA ROBERTS**

170 Shopping With: Serena Williams; Game, Set, Dress Me In Leather **BY GINIA BELLAFANTE**

173 Her U.S. Open Loss Behind Her, Serena Williams Turns to Fashion **BY VALERIYA SAFRONOVA**

175 Serena Williams Gives Birth to a Baby Girl **BY MATT STEVENS**

177 For Serena Williams, Childbirth Was a Harrowing Ordeal. She's Not Alone. **BY MAYA SALAM**

180 In This Sports Gender Gap, Men Fall Short BY WILL LEITCH

184 'I Won't Be Silent': Serena Williams on the Fear of Driving While Black BY CHRISTINE HAUSER

188 Away From Main Stages, a Victorious Serena Williams Sees Inequality BY CHRISTOPHER CLAREY

191 Serena Williams: Why Tennis Needs the Miami Open
BY SERENA WILLIAMS

194 Starring Serena Williams as Herself BY CHRISTOPHER CLAREY

203 The Meaning of Serena Williams BY CLAUDIA RANKINE

211 Glossary
212 Media Literacy Terms
214 Media Literacy Questions
216 Citations
222 Index

Introduction

ON MANY OCCASIONS throughout her professional career, Serena Williams has proven herself to be the best female tennis player in the world. She earned the top ranking in the Women's Tennis Association (WTA) eight times between 2002 and 2017, won twenty-three Grand Slam singles titles and fourteen doubles titles (Grand Slam tournaments being the Australian Open, the French Open, Wimbledon and the U.S. Open) and received four Olympic gold medals. She holds the record for the most singles titles won by a player in the current tennis era and may soon surpass the all-time record of twenty-four wins.

Since she was a child, Williams knew she wanted to be a tennis star. She was born in 1981 in Saginaw, Michigan, and began playing tennis when she was just four years old. She was homeschooled by her father, Richard Williams, who also coached Williams and her sister, Venus, and played an active role in nurturing their talent. Williams was raised a Jehovah's Witness, and aspects of her religious upbringing continue to impact her to this day.

Williams was eager to follow her older sister into professional tennis, and they would frequently meet on the court as rivals in singles and teammates in doubles in the following years. In 1995, when Serena was only fourteen, she attempted to make her professional debut in the WTA but was prevented from doing so because of age restrictions. Though she initially planned to challenge these restrictions in court, she ultimately waited until later in the year to compete in her first WTA tournament. Although she didn't become a part of the main WTA tour until 1998, she broke into the top ten in 1999, the same year she won the U.S. Open for the first time. Her meteoric rise proved that she wasn't merely Venus's little sister, but a talented player in her own right.

DAMON WINTER/THE NEW YORK TIMES

Serena Williams in 2018.

Despite Williams's many accomplishments, her professional career has had its ups and downs. After becoming the top-ranked player in 2002, Williams was forced to undergo knee surgery in 2003, after which she took an eight-month break from tennis. Upon returning to the tour she struggled to compete and fell out of the top ten. Furthermore, sports commentators and fans accused her of being out of shape and lacking commitment to the sport, and many speculated that she would retire from tennis. Williams, however, had other ideas, and in 2009 she returned to number one.

Between 2013 and 2015 Williams reached the zenith of her career, earning the number one ranking in 2013 and maintaining it through 2014 and 2015. She won every Grand Slam tournament between the 2012 Wimbledon and the 2015 Wimbledon. After her 2017 Australian Open victory it was revealed that Williams won while eight weeks pregnant, and she subsequently took an extended break to focus on her pregnancy and newborn daughter, Alexis Olympia Ohanian.

Williams returned to tennis in early 2018 as an unseeded player, but managed to make it to the Wimbledon finals nonetheless.

Williams has fascinated the public for reasons beyond her exceptional tennis skills. She is known for fashion choices on the court and consequently has collaborated with various apparel brands — including Puma and Nike — and has run her own lines of apparel and accessories. She has also won the admiration and friendship of various celebrities, and her 2017 wedding to Reddit co-founder Alexis Ohanian featured many high-profile guests, including Beyoncé and Kim Kardashian West.

Extending her influence beyond the tennis court, Williams uses her platform to address various issues that are important to her. She has spoken out about driving while black, unequal pay for and treatment of women — and particularly black women — in tennis, the lower quality of health care received by pregnant black women of all income brackets, and numerous other issues.

Williams is responsible for ushering in a new era in tennis, breaking records and taking a stand on some of the most pressing contemporary political and social issues. She has changed how tennis is viewed by the public and become a role model in the process, breaking down barriers for a new generation of athletes. This volume explores the many sides of Williams as a top athlete and celebrity, exploring the complexities of her long and storied life in the spotlight.

CHAPTER 1

Early Career and Stardom

Serena Williams made her professional debut at the age of 14 in 1995. Since then, she has battled Justine Henin, Kim Clijsters, Jennifer Capriati, Martina Hingis and her own older sister, Venus, to ascend to the top of the Women's Tennis Association. Some questioned whether she could possibly be as good as Venus or if she was too young and immature to be a top tennis pro. In 1999 Serena became a top-ten player, and in 2003 she won four consecutive Grand Slams, proving herself a star even at an incredibly young age.

Teen-Ager, Fighting to Turn Pro at 14, Puts Off Lawsuit for Now

BY ROBIN FINN | **OCT. 6, 1995**

FOR A WHILE it appeared Serena Williams, the younger sister of the phenom Venus, was about to start her own tennis career this month with a real bang: by filing an antitrust lawsuit against the women's tour because its age eligibility rules prohibit her from turning professional at age 14 the way her famous sister did a year ago.

It was originally Serena's mission to finagle herself a wild-card entry into the $430,000 Bank of the West Classic starting Oct. 30 in Oakland, Calif. This is the very event where the 327th-ranked Venus, who has a multimillion-dollar contract with Reebok, made a two-round professional splash in 1994 and will play her third and final event for 1995.

But Serena, who turned 14 last week, did so without enlisting the family's attorney, Kevin Davis, to take up legal arms against Oakland or the WTA Tour. According to Davis, Serena's decision not to sue for the right to play for pay at 14 is only temporary and was reached at the behest of her parents.

"I begged her to wait eight months to a year before she makes her move," said Richard Williams, the girls' father and president of their corporation, the Fantastic Company.

"We will not ask for a wild card in Oakland," he confirmed yesterday from Florida, "but if she does back off and wait, I think the WTA Tour should give her a break next year."

Nothing doing, said Anne Worcester, head of the women's tour.

"There will be no exceptions made," said Worcester, who explained to Serena this summer that the age-eligibility restrictions were made in order to protect young players and promote longer, healthier careers.

The same "phase-in" rule that allowed Venus to turn pro last year at 14 permits Serena to be treated like a 15-year-old this year, eligible to play four International Tennis Federation "futures" events and four small-scale tour events.

Serena, who has enrolled with Venus at a private school near their Palm Beach Gardens home, has indicated no interest in competing at any level except the top level.

LOPSIDED PAY SCALE

The WTA Tour reacted with outrage yesterday to an Australian Open plan that raises 1996 prize money to a record level of $9 million, but not at an equal level for the men's and women's fields.

While each singles champion will receive $562,000, the total prize money for men will increase by 17 percent while the total prize money for women will increase by just 6 percent. Only the women's champion and runner-up are scheduled to receive the 17 percent raise available to all male competitors.

"Australia has thrown gender equity out the window," said Worcester, who called the proposed prize structure "completely unacceptable."

A Family Tradition at Age 14

BY ROBIN FINN | OCT. 31, 1995

AFTER 10 YEARS of practice and a harrowing 15-hour trip through stormy skies, Serena Williams, the last of the 14-year-olds to sneak onto the women's tennis circuit, touched down at an obscure tournament over the weekend and, ostensibly without the blessing of her parents or the WTA Tour, began her professional career.

It was in all respects, from racquets to results, a lost weekend, and for the excited teen-ager from California, it was a weekend too long in the making. To those less trusting in the power of prodigies, it was a weekend that came much too soon.

Serena Williams has been described as everything from a fireball to a pit bull to a classically muscled natural athlete with a fierce netside manner. Family members profess to being a little afraid of her, especially on the court, where she is at her most unpredictable. Here at an unflashy event, she even vaulted the net with the aplomb of a practiced hurdler when her first-ever match, which took less than an hour, ended early last Saturday evening at the Club Advantage.

But it ended, as dreams sometimes do, in defeat.

"I felt bad out there because I lost," said Williams. "I didn't play like I meant to play. I played kind of like an amateur."

This was a debut far humbler than the splashy one her sister, Venus, made a year ago in the main draw of a top-level tournament in Oakland, Calif., where she drew top-seeded Arantxa Sanchez Vicario. Women's tennis, sobered by the crash-and-burn tale of its most spectacular ingenue, Jennifer Capriati, has since outlawed 14-year-olds from its mainstream events.

So the youngest Williams had to settle for the tennis version of an opening night tryout Off-Off-Off Broadway — the qualifying round of the Bell Challenge, to which she was admitted via a wild card granted on the basis of her renown rather than results.

Her saga began ominously.

A missed flight in Philadelphia, where she and her father, Richard, spent too much time hunting down souvenirs in the airport gift shop, left them scrambling to get to Canada. Somewhere along the journey that took father and daughter to four different airports, most of her racquets were lost in the shuffle. By the time they reached Quebec Friday night, it was bedtime, and there was no time for practice.

The professional unveiling of Serena Williams was a modest affair: 10 years of practice for this?

Instead of a stadium showcase, she competed on a regulation practice court at a tennis club in suburban Vanier, side by side with another qualifying match.

There were no spotlights, no introductions, not even any fans. Her court was set a level below a smoky lounge that held a bar, a big-screen television, an ice cream cart and 50 or so onlookers with varying stages of interest in her fate.

Welcome to qualifying where, to be truthful, she was not exactly welcomed by her lesser-sung peers.

Williams's high voltage reputation — as the unproven but ballyhooed sequel to last season's Venus phenomenon, as an iconoclastic prodigy who skipped the customary preparation provided by the juniors circuit, as a litigious upstart who threatened to sue the WTA for not allowing her to join her sister in the big leagues at Oakland this week — preceded her, particularly in the mind of her 18-year-old opponent.

"I guess I played a celebrity," said seventh-seeded Anne Miller, who chose not to be impressed and throttled Williams carefully from the baseline, 6-1, 6-1. Williams held serve only once and, although her abundance of raw talent was evidenced in her kamikaze returns — "She put her whole body into them," Miller observed — she broke Miller only once. She also constantly left herself out of position and vulnerable during their rallies.

"She has as much power as anybody around, but maybe she needs to play some junior events the way Anna Kournikova has to learn how to become match-tough," said Miller. "There really is no substitute for the real thing. I felt like a complete veteran compared to her."

She was.

But Williams, supported by her father, who has dismissed Rick Macci as tutor to his dual prodigies and is back to coaching them himself, still has no plans to pursue a conventional tennis education on the junior circuit. In fact, she said she probably won't compete again until she turns 15 next September. Then, under the same sleight of rule that allowed her to enter this Tier 3 Quebec event, she can use a wild card to gain admission to top-echelon events.

"I've practiced tennis since I was 4, and I practiced to play on the professional tour level, not the amateur, not the Tier 3 or 4 events," she said. "I feel like I'm more ready than ever to get out here and compete with the professionals. Once I make a decision, I never go back on it."

According to both of the Williams parents, neither Venus nor Serena turned professional as the result of a unanimous family decision.

"I wanted them to wait until they were 16," said the mother, Oracene Williams, who chaperoned 15-year-old Venus this week in Oakland. "I worry about them starting out quick and fizzling out early, but I'm trying to become immune to it, I guess."

At Oakland, Venus faced a veteran 20 years her senior, 215th-ranked Ros Nideffer, Monday night in the first round.

"I'm just afraid, especially with Serena, who's a perfectionist, that she'll take it so seriously that she'll never have fun with it, be a flop at 18," said Richard Williams. "I'm afraid that if she blows it and doesn't have a good time, she could end up with the same dysfunctions as Jennifer Capriati."

His apprehension notwithstanding, Williams was ready with an answer to why, if he and his wife disapprove of the dangers inherent in letting 14-year-olds gate crash the tennis workplace, both of his daughters wound up doing precisely that.

"You can't really say no to these kids these days, not the way parents did in my day," he said, as he gathered up his ninth-grader's gear, "and to be honest, if I did, I'm afraid I'd lose them."

Instead, father and daughter walked out of Club Avantage hand in hand, alone together, and hurried back to the hotel to reserve for Serena a flight to Oakland and the ongoing travails of Venus.

By Knocking Spirlea Out, Serena Williams May Get to Face Her Sister Next

BY ROBIN FINN | JAN. 19, 1998

MELBOURNE, AUSTRALIA — They are the hottest novelty act in this tennis-crazed city, and the act heated up on schedule today at the Australian Open.

Serena Williams, 16, pulled off a major opening-day upset to set up a possible second-round match with her 17-year-old sister, Venus. Playing on center court, Serena defeated sixth-seeded Irina Spirlea of Romania, 6-7 (5-7), 6-3, 6-1. Venus played her first-round match against 68th-ranked Alexia Dechaume-Balleret later today.

The Williamses' sister act is getting more complicated than the elaborate weave of beads and braids in the identical, inimitable hairdos that make anonymity a shared impossibility. While Venus and Serena insist that sibling rivalry is a foreign concept to them, on or off the tennis court, their first visit to Australia has put them on collision courses in two tournaments. For one sister to survive, there was the possibility she would have to eliminate the other.

If it seems a little unnatural, well, it is. Venus and Serena are clearly each other's best friend. But because there is no room for a best friend at the pinnacle of this profession, they have decided to be each other's best enemy, too.

That thought caused both of them, sitting on a sofa in a hotel lobby Sunday on the eve of their Australian Open initiations, to shrug their beaded heads, producing a muted clatter like a rattlesnake's warning note.

Though their mother, Brandy, who has taken over coaching duties here from her husband, Richard, had misgivings about her daughters' going one-on-one in their sworn pursuit of No. 1, the Williams sisters think they can handle this novelty, too.

"I wouldn't want to see Serena not succeed; that would be selfish of me," said Venus, who is ranked 16th. "I always knew that Serena would be my main nemesis one day."

Today, when Serena made her first Grand Slam singles appearance, the enemy, though familiar, was not a family member. She was a family antagonist: Spirlea, the player involved in the infamous body-bump with Venus before losing to her in the United States Open semifinals last year. Now it was the 53d-ranked Serena's turn to out-hustle her vast superior in the ranking, and she accomplished it with an increasingly vehement shellacking of Spirlea that featured no change-over fisticuffs but ample fist-brandishing from the excited victor.

The sisters said they had always understood that their day of sibling reckoning would come, but, abetted by this tournament's draw, it may come along a little sooner than either expected.

"It's pretty ironic," Serena had observed, before her match today, of a draw that pitted her against her big sister in the second round — but only if she first upset Spirlea. Spirlea got her revenge against Venus by trouncing her in straight sets at the Advanta Championships in November.

As for grudges, Serena said she did not think there was one between her and Spirlea.

"She wouldn't want to lose to me, and I don't blame her," Serena said. "No one wants to go out in the first round. That's the worst thing. I respect her, she has a wonderful forehand, but I have to respect myself, too. Playing the top seeds is the way to get my ranking better, and if anything, Spirlea has everything to lose and I don't."

Losing to her sister was not in Serena's plans, either.

"What's love got to do with it?" she said, joking about the prospect of upsetting her sister. "I don't have time to come along slowly; we both want to be No. 1, and I think it depends on whichever of us is more serious about it."

Last week, the Williams girls started out safely enough on opposite sides of the draw in the Sydney International.

But a high-stakes clash in the final was averted when Serena lost her semifinal against Arantxa Sanchez Vicario, who then beat Venus.

"Arantxa played well; it's not easy to get through two Williamses in the same week," Venus said.

Though some players criticized her for her bold prediction that she can get the No. 1 ranking later this year if her game improves on cue, Venus refused to retract it. But she said that her sister's swift transition from a trusted practice partner and supporter to a potential threat might put a crimp in her dreams.

"I always believed it would be me or Serena at No. 1; I just thought I'd get there before her, and she'd have to take it away from me," Venus said. "I wouldn't mind Serena taking it away from me as long as I could say I'd been there."

Serena Williams Leaves Her Mark on Davenport

BY ROBIN FINN | **MARCH 8, 1999**

NOW THAT SHE has developed the confidence to match her muscles, Serena Williams has declared her intention of shouldering into the top five by the year's end. After all, the year's beginning has produced her first career title, collected last week in Paris, and a significant victory over the world's No. 2 player, earned this afternoon in her debut appearance in the Evert Cup's singles draw.

Intent on outgrowing her role as understudy in the sister act she and her fifth-ranked sibling, Venus, have unleashed on the women's tour, Williams used her blistering returns and unbreakable serve to throttle last year's runner-up, second-seeded Lindsay Davenport, 6-4, 6-2.

Davenport has struggled through two courses of antibiotics trying to tame a virus she caught at the Australian Open in January and was neither sharp nor strong enough to contend with the power that Williams, ranked 21st and unseeded here, hurled across the net in the second-round match.

"She definitely took advantage of a good day to beat a top player," said Davenport, who had a chance to reclaim the No. 1 ranking from Martina Hingis had she been able to capture this event, her first in a month because of her illness.

Instead, Williams slipped ahead in their career rivalry, 2-1, and has no cause, she said, to be intimidated by Davenport or anyone else.

"If I'm playing well, doing the best that I can do, I'm definitely going to be in the top 10 and probably the top five, if not better," Williams said.

She said she used last year's defeat of Davenport in Sydney, Australia, as incentive to plow into this match not as an underdog, but as a clear threat.

"I was really mentally focused, and I really was mentally there," said Williams, who demonstrated her perseverance by flinging herself to the court in successful pursuit of a drop shot from Davenport in the final game. Williams catapulted from the backcourt to the net, scooped up the ball as her body scraped the hardcourt and collected a forehand winner. The move put Davenport deeper in trouble, down by 5-2, 15-30.

"Not too many other players probably would have gotten there; she is just a great athlete," Davenport said.

To punctuate her upset, Williams stabbed both arms into the air with a mix of menace and jubilation after her crosscourt forehand secured the victory. Then she raced to the corner of the court to embrace her father, Richard, whose recent strategy for making both daughters bona-fide world beaters, entering them in separate events when possible, appears to be reaping immediate rewards.

When Serena Williams won her inaugural title last Sunday by defeating the hometown heroine, the Australian Open runner-up Amelie Mauresmo, at the Gaz de Paris, Venus Williams was busy defending her first title in Oklahoma City.

"We played a lot of the same tournaments last year and it just didn't work," said Serena Williams, who picked up no titles while her sister won three in 1998. "If something isn't working, let's try something different. That's what we're doing."

The sisters are playing doubles together here, with Venus sitting out singles, but both have entered the Lipton Championships, later this month in Key Biscayne, Fla.

Serena Williams Will Put Streak on Line Against Hingis

BY ROBIN FINN | MARCH 25, 1999

UNSTOPPABLE, UNBEATABLE AND, at least for now, unapologetic about treating her superiors in the pecking order like stepping stones toward her sudden success at 17, Serena Williams extended her tour-best unbeaten streak to 15 matches with a 6-4, 6-0 demolition of ninth-seeded Amanda Coetzer of South Africa tonight at the Lipton Championships.

The 61-minute demonstration of power and precision tennis from the 16th-seeded Williams, who won the first two titles of her career at Paris and Indian Wells, Calif., heading into this event, delivered the teen-ager to a highly anticipated semifinal clash with top-ranked Martina Hingis of Switzerland. Hingis is one of the dwindling number of top-echelon players whom Williams — whose older sister, Venus, is the defending champion here — has yet to master. Hingis, who survived two match points to defeat Serena Williams in the quarterfinals here a year ago, leads their rivalry, 2-0.

"I'll have a lot of business to deal with out there," Williams said of her coming assignment. "She's No. 1; I'm No. 16. I've got nothing to lose."

But Williams hinted that she did not consider the taming of Hingis as her ultimate tennis test. That hurdle, she said, is represented by her older sister, another player she has yet to beat in the pros.

Tonight, Williams broke Coetzer in the eighth game of the first set to take a 5-3 advantage, failed to serve for the set, but rebounded by breaking Coetzer for the set with a blistering backhand drive that pinged harmlessly off the South African's outstretched racquet. Once Williams had asserted herself in the first set, she enjoyed carte blanche in the second; according to her, the reason for her current invincibility is a mature approach to her profession.

"Last year I had my goals set too high for me to reach; this year I just said to win one match at a time," she said. "Last year I was young; this year I guess you can say I'm old."

Like Williams, Hingis enjoyed a straight-set segue to the semifinals. Alternately buffeted and bolstered by a capricious summer breeze on the stadium court during the day session, Hingis hit her way into the semifinals with a brisk 6-1, 6-1 dissection of Barbara Schett of Austria. While the 20th-ranked Schett, who reached this round by ousting last year's runner-up, Anna Kournikova, did more missing than hitting in the shifting conditions, Hingis coped like a chameleon.

"You feel from one side like a weight lifter and from the other so easy and loose," Hingis said.

The Lipton's champion in 1997, Hingis was doubly ambushed here last year by the Williams sisters. After being worn to a frazzle and needing to save match points against Serena Williams in the quarterfinals, she was pummeled by Venus Williams in the semifinals. Hingis said she would relish the opportunity to test herself against Serena Williams in the semifinals on Friday.

"I'd love to play against Serena again," Hingis said. "I think everybody has improved since last year."

Hingis's one-sided quarterfinal lasted just 43 minutes today and was hustled along by Schett's six double faults and half-dozen dropped service games.

"I missed a lot of shots," Schett said. "Especially my serve was really bad. And without a serve, you can't beat the No. 1, for sure."

Though the men's top-seeded player, Carlos Moya of Spain, is long gone from this tournament, 74th-ranked Sebastien Grosjean of France, who knocked Moya from contention in the fourth round, costing Moya his new No. 1 ranking, is still a contender. He dismissed 40th-ranked Dominik Hrbaty in the quarterfinals, 6-3, 5-7, 6-1.

The Frenchman will next face 30-year-old Francisco Clavet of Spain, who is ranked No. 22 and is the oldest man in the field. Clavet beat Nicolas Kiefer of Germany, 7-5, 6-3, tonight.

In Thursday's other semifinal, seventh-seeded Richard Krajicek, who drilled Pete Sampras into a premature exit, will meet 14th-seeded Thomas Enqvist of Sweden.

It's 3 Sets and Pout for Serena Williams

BY ROBIN FINN | **MARCH 29, 1999**

SHE HAD NO CONTROL of her shots during her match and no control of herself after it ended. Serena Williams exited the center court at Roland Garros today to the tune of Gallic boos, not sympathy, after throwing a tiny temper tantrum in response to being upset by Mary Joe Fernandez, 6-3, 1-6, 6-0.

More of a farce than the force she had planned on being on the red clay at her second French Open, Williams used her racquet to apply a roundhouse punch to her wooden changeover chair after Fernandez used her racquet in a more conventional manner and thumped her out of the tournament. The chair and racquet survived, but the crowd condemned her fit of pique, a tempest the 17-year-old Williams described as just another personal double fault on a day littered with them.

"There was no excuse for the way I played today, really," said the 10th-seeded Williams, who made 26 of her 42 unforced errors in the opening set and unraveled completely in the third set, in which she won just 10 points. Near the dismal end, Williams pumped out a double fault, her sixth, to trail, 5-0.

"I should have been taken off the court and immediately asked to leave the facilities, never to return again," said Williams, who was positioned to meet her older sister, the fifth-seeded Venus, in the semi-finals. "In all actuality, I had planned on doing very well here, even taking the title. I never even dreamed in my wildest nightmares that I would have went out in the third round."

But out she went, a victim of her own errors and the insistent, penetrating ground strokes launched by the 37th-ranked Fernandez, who at 27 appears to be enjoying a renaissance two years after wrist surgery that had her mulling retirement.

"I always had my best results on clay, always played well here; I have good memories here," said Fernandez, who reached the final in 1993 and next plays the defending champion, Arantxa Sanchez Vicario.

Although Fernandez had never played Williams before, her morning warm-up partner, Martina Hingis, had predicted that Williams would lose today and provided Fernandez with a slew of insider information on the teen-ager's on-court vulnerabilities. Fernandez exploited them all, particularly Williams's footwork.

Besides keeping her shots deep, a strategy that prevented Williams from attacking with her typical fist-raised fervor, Fernandez directed her ground strokes to the corners, a tactic that kept Williams on the run, scuttling around the backcourt like a gerbil trapped on an exercise wheel.

"This is definitely the best win I've had all year," said Fernandez, who described the Williams sisters as the future.

"They're here already, but they're the future of our game," she said.

But on this present day, Williams played and behaved like a novice. "I was out of control," she acknowledged. "In practice, I was making my shots, but in the match, they were all going out or going into the net. If my thing is not working, I'm going to have to learn how to do something in order to make it work. My clay days are over for this year."

So are the clay days of seventh-seeded Tim Henman of Britain, a Sampras-esque serve-and-volley strategist who found himself in the position of being able to lay claim to the No. 1 ranking if he did the improbable and won this title. Instead, Henman did the wrong sort of improbable, squandered a two-sets-to-none lead and was ousted, 4-6, 4-6, 6-4, 7-5, 6-4, by 97th-ranked Alberto Berasategui, a Spaniard who discovered his Roland Garros comfort zone in 1994 as the runner-up to Sergi Bruguera.

Henman's countryman, 12th-seeded Greg Rusedski, has said there is a greater chance of extraterrestrials touching down in Britain than of his winning a French Open. But today he got halfway there, the first

British player to do so in 22 years, with a 6-2, 7-6 (9-7), 6-2 defeat of the Italian Davide Sanguinetti.

The resurgent Andre Agassi, seeded 13th, throttled the man who beat him here three years ago, Chris Woodruff of Knoxville, Tenn., 6-4, 6-4, 6-3. Agassi thus earned the highest-profile Round of 16 assignment, a date with the defending champion, Carlos Moya. "It's a good opportunity for me to step up my level of play and play my best tennis in the bigger situations," said Agassi, the lone American man left in the field.

"I don't think I could be a punching bag for five sets against anybody," he said about handling Moya's topspin, "but if I'm hitting my shots and controlling the points, I'll make five sets a concern for him."

The highest-seeded man left, No. 3 Patrick Rafter of Australia, downed the Frenchman Nicolas Escude, 7-5, 6-0, 2-6, 6-4, to remain on track to grab this title and the No. 1 ranking.

U. S. Open; Serena Williams Wins Match, Then Takes a Shot at Hingis

BY SELENA ROBERTS | SEPT. 3, 1999

SERENA WILLIAMS GLANCED down, pouted her lips and surveyed the size of her mouth. Not big, not big at all.

This did not match the measurement Martina Hingis made on Wednesday when she described the Williams family as having a "big mouth." But Williams assured everyone yesterday that there was an explanation for Hingis's assessment.

"She's always been the type of person that ... says things, just speaks her mind," Williams said. "I guess it has a little bit to do with not having a formal education. But you just have to somehow think more; you have to use your brain a little more in the tennis world."

They're so cute at this age. Here was the 17-year-old Williams, one hour removed from pulling the ponytail of the qualifier Jelena Kostanic, 6-4, 6-2, in the second round of the United States Open, and now she was blistering a return to the 18-year-old Hingis. While these two have all but shouted out "Food Fight!" on the pristine grounds of the National Tennis Center, a rather civilized and orderly Day 4 unfolded yesterday.

After fourth-seeded Monica Seles hustled past Silvia Farina, 6-2, 6-3, second-seeded Lindsay Davenport needed just 45 minutes to beat Ruxandra Dragomir, 6-0, 6-2. There was only a minor shake-up among seeded women's players when a lively Magui Serna, ranked No. 42 in the world, upset 14th-seeded Sandrine Testud, 6-3, 6-3. Testud, the first of the seeded women to fall, was admittedly flat and fatigued from a rigorous schedule.

"I've been playing the last six weeks in a row," Testud said. "I didn't stop, so I feel like it was a little bit too much for me."

On the men's side, in a draw that has taken a hit from the injury departures of Pete Sampras and Patrick Rafter, normalcy was restored when second-seeded Andre Agassi flicked away the qualifier Axel Pretzsch like lint off his sleeve, 6-3, 6-2, 6-1.

Agassi symbolized a day of simplicity for all the seeded men on the schedule. Twelfth-seeded Richard Krajicek and 15th-seeded Nicolas Kiefer also won easily. Only 10th-seeded Marcelo Rios dropped a set, but he rallied to beat George Bastl, 4-6, 6-3, 6-2, 6-3.

When night fell, though, an injury had forced another top player to withdraw. Eighth-seeded Carlos Moya retired in the third set of his match against Nicolas Escude, apparently because of a back injury, trailing by 1-6, 4-6, 1-0.

When Serena Williams slipped behind the dais in the interview room she opened up as if she were in bloom. She gladly described how she is more extroverted and how her sister, third-seeded Venus Williams, is more introverted. And she let everyone in on her current plans, like learning Portuguese and dabbling in fashion design.

"I'm into wedding dresses," she said. "I'm trying to add color to wedding dresses. I mean pure white, but with trims. I mean with a lavender, even a black and red, burgundy trim around it. I think that would be really nice."

As she spoke, she exuded an effervescent personality that was nearly carbonated. But there is the other side, like the articulate but cunning way she can race to return a dig against an adversary like Hingis.

But who started this? Hingis's remarks on Wednesday were in response to Richard Williams and his pre-Open prediction that the Williams sisters would meet in the final. In character, the brazen Hingis did not hold back when she said: "They always talk a lot. It's more pressure on them. Whether they can handle it or not, now that's the question."

Serena Williams handled it, all right. She had an answer or two for Hingis as her father, Richard, sat back and seemed to savor the ruckus.

"I don't think there's more pressure on them," Richard Williams said yesterday before his daughters played their doubles match. "I think pressure is doing what I did, working 9 to 5. I still believe there will be two Williamses in the finals.

"What Martina said is not a shock. I think she has the right to say what she wants to say. I'm going to ask her for her autograph. I love her. If you see her, tell her I love her."

Sure thing. But love was not in the air at his daughter's news conference. As Serena Williams beamed while discussing the moment she received her high school diploma, she slipped in a sly aside at an opponent she could soon face if the two meet in the final.

"I was pretty excited when I got my diploma," Williams said. "A lot of people can't say that, but I guess they pursue other things. In a way, I guess it's better for them. For instance, like Martina Hingis, she was No. 1 when she was 16. That's something I've never done personally. I still haven't won a Grand Slam and she's won five. She's pursued other things, and I'm pursuing education. I'm catching up in tennis, though." And then Williams smiled, bared her teeth and all but hissed.

"Obviously, she's No. 1, so she can say whatever she would like to say," Williams said, summing up her response to Hingis. "I personally don't think my mouth is big, if you're just looking at it."

MATCH POINTS

VENUS WILLIAMS received a walkover into the fourth round after her opponent, HENRIETA NAGYOVA, withdrew with a wrist injury.

U.S. Open; Serena Williams Sizes Up Seles, and Wins

BY ROBIN FINN | SEPT. 9, 1999

BIGGER, BETTER, BOLDER: that's been the fight song of 17-year-old Serena Williams ever since she shadowed her older sister — third-seeded Venus, who gate-crashed the 1997 United States Open final on her first try — into the Grand Slam spotlight.

Now the little sister has pronounced herself ready for Grand Slam prime time, ready to dethrone the Open's defending champion, Lindsay Davenport, in tomorrow's semifinals.

Last night the Open's spotlights were trained on seventh-seeded Serena, whose final-round collision course with Venus became a less-than-distant possibility when Serena reached the first Grand Slam

CLIVE BRUNSKILL/GETTY IMAGES SPORT

Serena Williams signs books for fans at the USTA National Tennis Courts in Flushing Meadows, New York, in September 1999.

semifinal of her career with a 4-6, 6-3, 6-2 comeback against fourth-seeded Monica Seles.

The energized Williams, so resilient on the baseline that Seles had trouble pounding the ball into nooks and crannies the teenager deemed unreachable, out-screeched and overpowered the two-time Open champion.

"Two years on the tour and I haven't done anything in the Slams; it's my turn," said a giddy Williams, who is 3-0 against Seles. "I have the attitude that I'm not going to lose."

With her white beads restrained in two pigtails but her imposing muscles on full display in her racer-back tennis costume, Williams betrayed few youthful jitters and ample aggression. As she did in her last few matches here at her second Open, Williams used the first set to size up her prey and the next two to pour on the pressure.

After pounding the tired Seles into a 5-2 final-set deficit, Williams used her 15th ace to gain triple match point, and converted her second match point with a 115-mile-an-hour service winner. The victory sent Williams into the semifinals against Davenport, who needed to save two match points to escape her quarterfinal with a 6-2, 3-6, 7-5 victory over fifth-seeded Mary Pierce.

Through the first four rounds, Davenport had scooted through her first Grand Slam title defense like a kid riding no-hands on a shiny two-wheeler: 6-foot-2-inch Davenport, who embellished her breakthrough United States Open crown with a Wimbledon championship this July, was back to being unbeatable after an August letdown.

But then came yesterday's harrowing quarterfinal, a rain-interrupted stadium ordeal in which Davenport's momentum hit a serious snag when she collided with a regal speed bump.

Suddenly Davenport — whose daydreams of back-to-back Open titles had been three rounds away from becoming a happy reality — was pacing the baseline with a frown on her face and two match points on Pierce's racquet. Suddenly she was as glum as the weather. Suddenly she had stage fright on her favorite stage.

"Anyone who says they don't get nervous is lying," said the second-seeded Davenport, who ultimately benefited when her opponent became more nervous than she was in this 2-hour-1-minute game of baseline chicken. Using torque as their tactic, each dared the other to back down first. Finesse was not a factor, but fitness was.

After Davenport ran Pierce off the court in the first set and Pierce claimed cruise control in the second, Davenport fended off two match points to break Pierce for 5-5 in the third, plopped down on a couch and pretended to relax through an hourlong rain delay, then sneaked into the semifinals when Pierce produced a billowing double fault at match point.

"I'm getting closer to defending, had a little stumble, but I'm still around," said the relieved Davenport, who out-aced Pierce by 9-5 and had no double faults. Pierce plunked out seven, the last of which came at the worst of times for her, a three-time Grand Slam finalist who captured her sole Grand Slam title at the 1995 Australian Open.

"Finally able to get a double fault, which is a sad way to end," said Davenport, who had sympathy for Pierce but wasn't about to request a more interesting display for her second match point. "I fought off a lot of game points in that game, so I'm happy. I'm excited the way I handled it."

There was rain spattering the Arthur Ashe Stadium as fifth-seeded Pierce, wearing a two-piece Lycra outfit and a three-plait braid, marched to the slippery baseline to serve for the upset, and her first spot in a United States Open semifinal, at 2-6, 6-3, 5-4.

Though Davenport put a sneaker to the line, watched her foot skid, and sent a quizzical glare in the direction of the chair umpire Dessie Samuels, play was not halted.

Pierce pasted a serve-and-forehand combination that sent her to match point, at 40-30. But Davenport nullified that by snapping a crosscourt backhand off the sideline. Pierce used a crosscourt forehand blast to set up a second match point, only to undermine it with a backhand approach that turned too boisterous as it crossed the net:

she turned angrily on her heel to try again for a third match point, but this time Davenport broke her, and the umpire halted the 5-5 stalemate by announcing a suspension of play.

"It was the right decision to stop play," said Pierce, who viewed her tough treatment of Davenport as a positive development. "I mean, she won this tournament last year. She's No. 2 in the world, was No. 1. I had two match points. This match probably motivates me more, opens my eyes to what I need to work on."

Such as her shot selection on match points. "You know, I'm human," she said. "I got a little bit nervous and a little tight."

Back on the court in the fading sunshine, Davenport started the 11th game with a pair of crisp, cruel aces, didn't fret when Pierce pushed her to deuce, and held for a 6-5 edge. In trouble on her serve, Pierce tackled a break and match point for Davenport by belting a forehand winner down the line.

But another overblown forehand from Pierce granted Davenport a match point, where all she had to do was await serve and play voyeur as Pierce's second serve strayed beyond bounds.

"I'm just lucky to be here; you have to go with that," she said of her quarterfinal escape. "Sometimes it just turns the tournament around, and you play even better."

U.S. Open; Little Sister Becomes the Stardust Half

BY ROBIN FINN | SEPT. 12, 1999

USING HER RACQUET like a stun gun to pound and paralyze her savvy opponent, the No. 1-ranked Martina Hingis, into submission yesterday, Serena Williams, the 17-year-old follow-up act to her big sister phenom, Venus, captured the women's championship at the United States Open in her first appearance in a Grand Slam final.

Williams's breakthrough, coupled with the advance of Andre Agassi and Todd Martin to the men's final, guaranteed the century's final Open a patriotic denouement, its first American-born champions since Jimmy Connors and Chris Evert prevailed in 1982.

"Oh, my God, I won, oh my God," the jubilant Williams mouthed, clasping both hands to her thumping heart, after Hingis motored a double-handed backhand out of bounds on Williams's third match point. That sealed a 6-3, 7-6 (7-4) upset for the youngest of the five Williams sisters, the one who calls herself the family extrovert. The victory moved Williams, who dethroned the Open's defending champion, Lindsay Davenport, in the semifinals, to a career-best fourth in the computer ranking, just behind her celebrated sibling, Venus, who has yet to win a Grand Slam title.

"It's really amazing; I was always the one who said, 'I want to win the U.S. Open,' and Venus, she always wanted Wimbledon," said Williams, who fielded a congratulatory call from President Clinton and his daughter, Chelsea. Williams said they talked tennis, not politics. "I'm not into politics," she said.

Her initial reaction to winning, Williams said, was a big blur. "I thought, 'Should I scream, should I yell or should I cry?' And I guess I ended up doing them all."

She will have another chance today when she and Venus play in the doubles final. The sisters won their semifinal last night, defeating Mary Pierce and Barbara Schett, 7-6 (7-2), 6-3.

The fifth-youngest champion in Open history, Serena Williams became the first African-American woman to reign supreme on a Grand Slam stage since Althea Gibson, who counted the 1957 and 1958 Opens among her five Grand Slam crowns, became the first black woman to claim a major title in 1956.

The last woman to win the Open on her first visit to its final was Hingis, who collected her third Grand Slam title of 1997 by defeating Venus Williams, then an unseeded and 66th-ranked neophyte with a little sister too young to compete on the tour.

But the 5-foot-10-inch, 145-pound Serena Williams, called the "better, badder, meaner" competitor of the talented pair by their father and coach, Richard, made a swift climb after turning professional at 15. In 1997 she moved from 453d to 99th in the ranking, in 1998 she won a pair of Grand Slam mixed doubles titles, and this spring she went on a 16-match rampage that yielded titles at Paris and Indian Wells, Calif., and carried her to an all-Williams finale at the Lipton Championships. Her current streak of invincibility stretched to 13 with yesterday's victory, her second consecutive upset of Hingis, whose record of futility when trying to defeat both Williams sisters at the same event remained intact — now 0-3.

"I was really mentally tough out there," said Williams, now 3-3 against Hingis. "I wouldn't give in to anything. The first set, I wanted to come out strong and tough and I did."

The seventh-seeded Serena Williams was less than lethal only when she fumbled away two match points as a desperate Hingis served at 3-5 of the second set. The glitch carried over and caused Williams to lose her composure as she stepped up to serve for the victory at 5-4 of the second set. As the topper to a mounting pile of unforced errors, Williams walloped a forehand long at triple break point that allowed the tenacious 18-year-old Swiss back into the thick of things.

"She was always leading, I felt like always being behind, being defensive, but I was reborn like, when she missed those two match points," said Hingis, who called the final stages of the match a willpower game.

With her mother, Melanie Molitor, back in her customary coaching corner after the debacle at Wimbledon, where Hingis's attempt at emancipation produced a tearful first-round loss, Hingis had reached her third Grand Slam final of 1999. She won just one of them, the Australian Open, but unlike the French Open, where her final against Steffi Graf deteriorated into a spiteful tantrum, she seemed undisturbed by yesterday's setback, her second consecutive defeat in an Open final.

"So far I'm still at the top," Hingis said. "I think all of us, we are pretty much at our limits; I don't think it can get much better," she said of the caliber of tennis played.

After Hingis held for a 6-5 edge, it was Williams's turn to scramble into a tie breaker. It took her five deuces, but she got there with a blistering down-the-line passing shot. While Williams wasn't happy with herself for tensing up on her two match points at 5-3 — she blew the first with a wild backhand that steered way clear of its sideline target and the second with a netted backhand return — Williams relaxed once she found herself in a tie breaker.

"I feel that I can't lose in tie breakers; that's when the serve really counts," said Williams, now 6-0 in 1999 tie breakers.

After Hingis leveled the tie breaker at 4-4 by angling a snarling crosscourt forehand over the net and forcing a forehand error from the panting Williams, the American snapped right back with an untouchable forehand down-the-line return that granted her a 5-4 edge. Another furious rally produced a defensive lob from Hingis that wafted over Williams's head and, just as she knelt in surrender after a frantic chase, touched down just behind the baseline to give her a third match point.

"I think after I lost those two match points I was very upset with myself," Williams said. "I thought for sure I was going to hold my serve at 5-4. I guess something went dreadfully wrong. There comes a time when you just have to stop caving. In the end, I told myself, 'You're going to have to perform.' That's what I did."

This time Williams had her work done for her by Hingis, who pumped a backhand long, unleashed a grimace in place of her usual Cheshire cat smirk, and waited for the winner to absorb her accomplishment. At net, they shared a brief hug, the most positive interaction of a two-week stint of sniping instigated by Richard Williams's prediction that both his daughters would reach the final. Hingis, who took exception to that, had called the Williams patriarch a bigmouth; Venus Williams, who fell to Hingis in the semifinals, stayed out of the fray, but Serena attributed Hingis's outburst to her "lack of formal education."

Yesterday, the battle lines were drawn up in shots, not verbiage: Williams, whose eight aces improved her Open total to 63, had 36 winners, while Hingis managed only seven.

"She was just better today," Hingis said. "Between Serena and me, the comments went back and forth, but at the end, it's just been terrific tennis."

Failing to Find Rhythm, Serena Williams Ousted

BY CHRISTOPHER CLAREY | JAN. 24, 2000

THE SURFACE WAS still green, hard and quick. The lines were still white. But the tennis that Serena Williams produced in this Grand Slam event bore little resemblance to the tennis she produced on her way to the title at Flushing Meadows in September.

There will be no surprised stumble along the baseline after match point on the final weekend; no phone conversation with President Clinton and his daughter, Chelsea. Williams made sure of that today in the fourth round of the Australian Open, where she beat herself as much as she was beaten by Yelena Likhovtseva.

The final score was 6-3, 6-3, and Williams, seeded third, looked sluggish and out of sorts for most of the match against the 16th-seeded Russian, who has an all-court game but rarely had to make full use of it against her gaffe-prone opponent.

Williams made 32 unforced errors: an average of nearly two a game. And it was altogether appropriate that her last shot of this surprisingly brief encounter was a backhand that struck the net for little apparent reason.

"There's no excuse for me to have lost this match," she said. "I couldn't find my rhythm throughout the match. It was strange."

Under normal circumstances, there might be another Williams still in the draw to keep tennis's first family in contention. But Serena's older sister Venus withdrew from this event shortly before it began, citing a wrist injury, and now there will be no beaded, seeded Floridians to occupy the opposition and the autograph seekers for the rest of the tournament.

Serena herself was uncertain whether she would play in this event in December. "I just changed my mind," she said last week. "I thought that if I didn't come that maybe my ranking would slip because I saw that Mary Pierce was coming up behind me."

That at least is no longer a worry. Pierce was upset in the fourth round by Ai Sugiyama on Sunday. But in a sense, Williams's indecision about playing here was reflected by her indecision on the court. She was pushed to three sets in her opening match by Amanda Grahame, a little-known Australian, and though she played better in the third round against Sabine Appelmans, she resumed struggling again today after taking a 3-1 lead.

She would lose eight games in a row against a player she had beaten in their only two previous meetings. And though she rallied from 0-3 to 3-3 in the final set, her wayward ground strokes soon had her trailing again for good. When it ended, she walked quickly off court in the flashy red-and-black dress that had been designed to be worn much longer in Melbourne than four rounds.

This is only the third event in which Williams has played since she defeated Monica Seles, Lindsay Davenport and Martina Hingis in successive matches to win the United States Open last fall. Her last match before this tournament was last October in Filderstadt, Germany, where she was beaten in the first round by Sandrine Testud. She later withdrew from the season-ending Chase Championships with a back injury. Her back troubled her again here in the first round, and she has been receiving daily treatment. But she insisted the injury had not been a factor against Likhovtseva.

The Williamses have made a habit of defying tennis convention. They played precious little junior tennis before turning professional, and are now coached by their parents, who are self-taught and never played the game at a high level. Serena defied convention again by not playing a warm-up event before the Open. But though she conceded earlier in the tournament that perhaps she had made a mistake, she rejected that suggestion completely today.

"I wasn't unprepared," she said. "I was here long enough. I answered that question a million times anyway. That's no excuse. I lost because I didn't play well, and she played good. I couldn't make any shots."

The other reigning United States Open singles champion, Andre Agassi, needed no excuses after his fourth-round victory over the Australian Mark Philippoussis. Agassi played remarkably controlled and clever tennis in the first two sets on Sunday and after he had rallied from a 4-1 deficit in the second-set tie breaker, the 16th-seeded Philippoussis, normally a mild-mannered sort despite his imposing physique, reared back and smashed his racket on the court.

"The guy can make a racket look like a toothpick you know," Agassi said. "I was just thinking, 'I'm glad I'm not the racket.' "

Agassi, the No. 1 seed, ended up winning by 6-4, 7-6 (7-4), 5-7, 6-3 to advance to the quarterfinals, where he will face Hicham Arazi of Morocco. Pete Sampras also advanced with a four-set victory over Slava Dosedel of the Czech Republic. Sampras could face Agassi in the semifinals, but first he must get past another American, Chris Woodruff, who upset 11th-seeded Tim Henman in five sets.

Nicolas Kiefer of Germany, seeded fourth, also reached the quarterfinals by defeating Wayne Ferreira in straight sets today. In the women's draw, Arantxa Sanchez-Vicario defeated Barbara Schett, 1-6, 6-0, 7-5, in the fourth round. Conchita Martinez also won, beating the American Kristina Brandi, 6-1, 6-1.

Sydney 2000: Tennis; Who Could Ask for Anything More?

BY SELENA ROBERTS | SEPT. 29, 2000

TEN DAYS AGO, Venus and Serena Williams arrived as two players in the Olympic medal mix, but they left today after overwhelming the scene like a dye drop in a pool.

Eventually, the Williams sisters spread their talents until they became the dominant vision on the medal stand. Just 24 hours after Venus Williams won a gold medal in singles, she joined her sister Serena, to take the gold for America in doubles.

"Our competition is over," Venus Williams said. "We can't do anything more."

Before it was over, Venus and Serena Williams created the buzz of the tournament. Without them, the draw would have come up short in style, flair and name value. Unlike Martina Hingis and others, the Williams sisters did not consider playing for their country too taxing on their schedule. Instead, they embraced the opportunity and found joy in the Olympic atmosphere.

Upon match point, Venus and Serena Williams tossed their rackets in the air, wrapped their arms around each other at the service line and hugged all the way to the net, where they greeted Miriam Oremans and Kristie Boogert, the Dutch pair they dismissed in 50 minutes.

"For me, this is almost bigger than singles," Venus Williams said. "It's right up there because I have this victory with Serena, my sister, my family member, my best friend."

Together, they left Oremans and Boogert all but pock-marked from the Williams mortar shots during the 6-1, 6-1 American victory.

"It has been fantastic here," Serena Williams said. "Just to win the gold medal, it has been a great thing for me and my family. We've worked so hard. It's great for everyone, for the whole U.S. team."

When United States Coach Billie Jean King assembled the women's team, the plan was to sweep the singles, as well as doubles. If Lindsay Davenport hadn't injured her foot, the United States might have delivered. As it was, Monica Seles won the bronze for the United States only after losing to Venus Williams in the semifinals, leaving only the silver in singles up for grabs. Russia's Elena Dementieva gladly grabbed it while she could.

In the background of the Williams sisters, the Russians were quietly asserting themselves as a world power in tennis. Although Marat Safin made an early exit in the men's draw, Dementieva backed up her coming out party at the United States Open with an encore at the Olympics. And although the men's draw was more threadbare of stars than the women's side, the Russian Yevgeny Kafelnikov found adrenaline from the sight of his country's flag and came up with a gold medal today in one of the best matches of the tournament.

By devouring short balls with swinging forehand winners, leaning on his big serve when faced with disaster, and being patient in the heat of every intense baseline rally, Kafelnikov outlasted Tommy Haas of Germany, 7-6 (4), 3-6, 6-2, 4-6, 6-3.

"When I lost the fourth set today, I talked to myself," Kafelnikov said. "I said, 'You have come all the way here to play the final match in the Olympics. If you lose the match, you are going to regret it the rest of your life.' And that's what kept me motivated."

There was not any shame in taking a silver back to Russia — which Kafelnikov was reminded of in a prematch telephone conversation with his wife, Mascha, and children — but he was inspired by the moment to win the gold.

The Williams sisters felt the same way. For almost two weeks, they were not individuals but part of a team. They were not being guided by their parents, but being coached by King and her assistant, Zina Garrison. As a result, there were some tweaks made in the Williams sisters' technique. Their volleys were sharper and their doubles movement was more synchronized.

"They listen very well," said King, who, along with Garrison, may continue some spot coaching of the sisters. "They really want to improve."

Right now, they are close to invincible. Any better, and the Williams sisters would be untouchable. As their Olympic competition ended, Venus Williams's singles winning streak stood at 32; and the sisters had won 33 of 34 doubles matches. Putting her name down in history, Venus Williams also became the first woman to win gold medals in the singles and doubles since Helen Wills in 1924. Tennis rejoined the Olympic program in 1988, after an absence of 64 years.

"Where we are right now is just good," Venus Williams said. "We have done everything we could at the Olympics. When we compete, we do all that we can. Even if it's a bad decision, we give it 110 percent. Right now, we are in a really good place."

MATCH POINTS

The Williams sisters were asked to respond to JOHN MCENROE's latest critique of them. In a British newspaper, McEnroe described the sisters as less than gracious in victory. "I don't think we are here to talk about that," SERENA WILLIAMS said. "I'm sure he's a great guy."

The United States women won the gold medal in singles and doubles for the third straight Olympics. In competitions where more than one gold is awarded, a country has swept the top award only three times in at least three consecutive Olympics. The most dominant team was the United States men's diving team, which swept all gold medals in 1924, 1928, 1932, 1936, 1948 and 1952.

Serena Williams Wins As the Boos Pour Down

BY SELENA ROBERTS | MARCH 18, 2001

ABOUT FIVE MINUTES before the match, a sun-kissed crowd known for its relaxed spirit spotted Richard and Venus Williams beginning a long walk down the 50 steps to their courtside perch.

Immediately, a crescendo of boos began ushering the father and daughter to their seats. Soon, the stadium was filled with the eerie howl found in haunted houses. Halfway to his destination, a defiant Richard Williams turned and shook his fist at his 15,000 critics.

All the while, revealing no sign of a limp, no wrap on her controversial right knee, Venus Williams kept her head down as she slipped into her row. They had arrived to see Serena Williams play 17-year-old Kim Clijsters in the final of the Tennis Masters Series Indian Wells, but they had stepped on the tripwires to the fans' emotions.

Few wanted to forgive Venus Williams for pulling out of her semifinal against her sister four minutes before the match on Thursday night. Her penchant for vanishing from tournaments had ruined her credibility. Few wanted to believe that her exit was not part of a fix conjured up by their father. His string of wild tales over the years has left his denials hollow.

Once Richard and Venus sat down, Serena Williams had to absorb the brunt of the fury. Her double faults became reason for celebration. Her shots into the net ignited cheers. But Serena Williams eventually channeled her frayed emotions into her game to take the title, 4-6, 6-4, 6-2.

"At first, obviously, I wasn't happy," Serena Williams said. "I don't think mentally I was ready for that. To be honest, what I literally did on a changeover, I prayed to God to help me be strong, not even to win, but to be strong, not listen to the crowd."

This spiritual search came during the second set. At that point, she began to play in an isolation booth, detached from the crowd.

Williams began to prey on Clijsters's inexperience. Clijsters, of Belgium, had beaten Martina Hingis to arrive in the final, but her composure was melting under Williams's power. On her last cathartic swing of the match, Williams punched a forehand crosscourt for a winner.

The celebration was awkward. As she began a parade queen's wave at the crowd, boos mixed with a smattering of applause.

"I'd like to thank everyone who supported me, and if you didn't, I love you guys anyway," Williams said after accepting her trophy and a winner's check for $330,000.

The day did not start out so hostile, or end without a cheer. Pete Sampras and Andre Agassi set up a meeting in Sunday's men's final, a matchup that will bring joy to anyone who wants to make a toast to longevity. Over 12 years, the two have met 29 times, with Sampras leading the series, 17-12.

At times, fate did not seem on the side of a Sampras-Agassi final. Early in the day, Sampras turned momentum around on Yevgeny Kafelnikov, who led then folded. Kafelnikov watched Sampras run off five games at the end of the first and second sets to win, 7-5, 6-4.

"I was quite impressed with his enthusiasm on the court today," Kafelnikov said. "I guess when you're getting older, when you feel like your time is running out, you've got to do that. That just shows he wants to play a lot longer."

This dip into the past had come full circle by nightfall, when Agassi pushed by in his semifinal, 6-4, 3-6, 6-4. The 30-year-old Agassi outlasted 20-year-old Lleyton Hewitt, who had been the lone survivor of the tour's "New Balls, Please," marketing campaign aimed at showcasing the post-Agassi-Sampras generation.

"I see myself around at least another five years," Sampras said.

Neither Sampras nor Agassi is going anywhere for now. In between the feel-good triumphs of Sampras and Agassi, the giddy California crowd stopped to get surly. Their response to the Williams family set up a surreal drama.

Serena Williams and Kim Clijsters of Belgium hold their trophies following the Tennis Masters Series final on March 17, 2001.

Suddenly embraced, Clijsters started the match by crushing a forehand down the line for a winner. As she jumped out to a 3-0 lead, Williams was visibly flustered by her role as the villain, even though she was not the sister who pulled out of the semifinal.

"How many people do you know who would go out and jeer a 19-year-old? Come on, I'm just a kid," said Serena Williams, who added, "I'm just an innocent person."

Slowly, she began to regroup in an atmosphere she described as chaos. But there was nothing aesthetically pleasing about the match. Clijsters had 31 unforced errors; Williams made 43.

"We played very aggressive tennis," Clijsters said. "That means we play with more unforced errors."

In the beginning, Clijsters's display of assertiveness was rewarded with a lead. After it was over, Clijsters's show of sympathy revealed why she won the tour's sportsmanship award.

"She's a very nice person," Clijsters said of Serena Williams. "I don't think it's up to the crowd to put pressure on her."

Still, the fans took sides. After being heckled by the crowd, Richard Williams was seen on his cellular phone. Minutes later, a security guard showed up by the friends' box a couple of games into the match.

There was no incident, though. The abuse landed in verbal blows. Richard Williams's prematch fist shake was his only reaction. When a reporter approached him afterward, he motioned for security. The father sought protection, but his daughter Serena had found redemption.

"I won a big battle today mentally," Serena Williams said. "I think a champion can come through."

Sports of The Times; Center Stage for Families and Dramas

BY HARVEY ARATON | JULY 4, 2001

IF PEOPLE HERE thought the royals were strange, they hadn't yet experienced an afternoon at Center Court with the Williamses and the Capriatis. Or in the contrived lexicon of all-American entertainment, "One Life to Live" meets "The Simpsons."

Two tennis prodigies from families that have historically been, well, different, commanded the sport's supreme stage here yesterday and created part confrontation and part cartoon. The fittingly bizarre finish was achieved after the player who committed a ghastly 75 unforced errors was 2 points away from victory and then, based on her own analysis of medicine and mind, coughed up the match.

"I have the chills; I have a horrible headache; I'm not alive right now," Serena Williams said after also contracting a malady not uncommon to these fraying lawns, miss-and-hit disease, and dropping her Wimbledon quarterfinal to Jennifer Capriati, the continually resurgent wonder, by 6-7 (4), 7-5, 6-3.

Capriati's Grand Slam pursuit is alive. The all-Williams final is not. This was a match that not-so-little sister Serena seemed to have on her racket, as long as she could keep the ball and herself in play. She ultimately succeeded more with the latter than with the former, though her stiff-legged and hasty postmatch departure did have the distinct look of someone who just had to go.

"I didn't want to know the details," Capriati said.

Nor was she interested in discussing Williams's labeling herself a hypochondriac, as opposed to a player merely plagued by bad health. Even though she was clearly distressed between many points, Williams credited Capriati for lifting her game. But Capriati said she has heard it all from Serena before, explanations for defeats that sounded too much like excuses.

"It's pretty much the same things that happen every time I played her," she said. "It doesn't matter. I think I know the truth inside. I think most people do."

Actually, it was no simple task to know what was happening during this wildly uneven match, and when. On the one hand, when Williams called for the trainer after the fifth game of the second set, she was not only up a set and a break but was playing through the long rallies as well as she can. On the other hand, she later withdrew from doubles, and the Women's Tennis Association confirmed that Williams wasn't feeling good before facing Maggie Maleeva in Monday's Round of 16.

Williams won that match, 6-2, 6-1, after which Maleeva said that while the Williams sisters must deal better with their Tour coexistence and potential showdowns, she could relate to their unusual reality, especially Serena's.

"I was the youngest of three sisters who all played tennis, and by the time I came along, everyone expected me to be good," she said. "I never did beat my sisters, and I never did appreciate my own success until I got hurt and couldn't play for more than a year."

What a dysfunctional family web women's tennis typically weaves, and nobody should know that better than Capriati, whose pushy father and tortured adolescence landed her in a dreadful cycle of self-immolation. Even yesterday, temporarily sagging, Capriati was tossing her racket and begging Papa Stefano with her eyes for a way to diffuse Williams's power. She twice needed medical attention for a sore hip.

It was one thing, then, for a judgmental California preppie like Lindsay Davenport to say it "looks like that" when asked if it seems as if Serena Williams won't accept an alibi-free defeat. Capriati, with the crowd overwhelmingly for her, might have been more sympathetic. She, more than anyone, should recognize that being a Williams sister can't be easy, given their father's eccentricities, reports of family tensions and the pressure of growing up in a public pressure cooker.

Serena Williams obviously has some growing up to do but who, at 19, does not? It was just two years ago that Capriati, already 23, wept uncontrollably at the United States Open while addressing her past. In the interview room yesterday, Williams's eyes glistened as she relived the crucial second set that got away, at which time Richard Williams brushed past the guard posted by the family box, never to return.

Thank you, Dad, coach and spiritual guide. Soon Richard was replaced by big sister Venus, who had dispatched Nathalie Tauziat in a match that began well after Serena's. By the time Venus appeared, Capriati was on a nine-game roll, about to move one victory away from the final and possibly another Capriati-Williams episode that could give us all chills.

CHAPTER 2

Mid-Career Trials and Triumphs

After earning her reputation as a tennis wunderkind, Serena Williams struggled to maintain her top ranking. In 2005 she fell out of the top ten, and her performance and ranking only declined from there. She suffered a series of injuries and was criticized by sports commentators for being out of shape and unfocused on her game. During this decline she was also faulted for being temperamental on and off the court, which was considered a sign of the emotional toll of her professional nadir. Despite these obstacles Williams managed to turn her tennis career around and regained her top ranking in 2009.

Serena Williams Needs Some of Agassi's Grit

BY SELENA ROBERTS | AUG. 30, 2006

ORACENE PRICE HAD just walked in from the rain, safe from skies shading the tennis grounds' nearly movie-theater dark, but, typically, she was wearing sunglasses, big and thick as Jackie O's shades.

So it's impossible to read the eyes of Serena Williams's mother. You're left to decode shoulder shrugs and smiles. At the very mention of Serena's mysterious spiral, on questions of her daughter's commitment and fitness and plunge in the rankings, Oracene stood up straight, her body language spelling out confidence.

"Serena is ready," she said with a knowing grin. "She's like, 'Bring it on.' "

Serena's first-round match at the United States Open was postponed because of the weather, but we'll know soon enough if she can find a path from the bottom, if she can discover an escape hatch from personal demons, if she has more than a little Andre Agassi in her.

Separated by a dozen years, but a whole tennis generation, the parallels between Agassi and Williams can be drawn from their splashy arrivals through the commonality of their career nadirs.

Agassi was, at first, celebrated as the perfect hair-band rocker to put tennis on the pop charts, a DayGlo corporate darling for anyone who dug distressed denim shorts, Zen and bottled blonds.

Remember what Cher did for Sonny? Andre Agassi delivered the everyman Pete Sampras a glamorous stage foil.

Then, years later, Agassi would be mocked, for indulging in Taco Bell and celebrity crushes, for his suspicious injuries, lapsed dedication and belly bulge. In 1997, at age 27, Agassi owned three majors, an unknown future and a No. 141 ranking.

"Someday, when he tells his grandkids about the majors, he will be able to tick them off: Nike, Canon, Mountain Dew," wrote Sports Illustrated.

Williams, at first, was glamorized as a tennis establishment gatecrasher in beaded braids who morphed into a confident woman comfortable on the catwalk and in cat suits on the court, daring in style and aggressive in play.

Remember what muscle did for Charles Atlas? Williams made superpower marketable on the women's tour.

Now, years later, Williams is punch-line fodder for critics who remark on her weight gain and tease her for having a caboose on the loose. She is often criticized for habitually withdrawing from tournaments with curious injuries, for putting her outside interests ahead of the Tour's interests, for her free fall in the rankings.

At the start of this summer, Williams was 24, owner of seven majors, but No. 139 on the Tour computer.

"Serena in particular is more involved with fashion shows and TV appearances than the practice courts, and has more about her (not just in the posterior department) than your average female tennis player," wrote The Daily Telegraph in Britain at the Australian Open.

What's a clever comeback to the jokes?

It's not easy to reply when hecklers seem out of touch with circumstances. Agassi had been through a tumultuous time between 1996 and 1997. He married the actress Brooke Shields, adding a new and complicated dimension to his life. Some called her a distraction.

Serena has been through a more critical change in her life. Almost three years ago, her half sister Yetunde was murdered on the streets of Compton, Calif. She has suffered loss, dealt with a lot of pain, sometimes disappearing from the Tour.

"We've had a lot of issues," Price said. "She has had to work through a lot of difficult things. We all have."

Life is more important than tennis. And Agassi learned how to bring balance to the two once he discovered tennis and perspective didn't have to be mutually exclusive.

Agassi rededicated himself. After he fell in the rankings, he played challenger events near public parks in Las Vegas and Burbank, Calif. More important, he reached out for help. He turned to his friend and trainer Gil Reyes for a path to mental and physical fitness. Within a year, Agassi was running the hills above his home in Las Vegas, pushing his pain threshold, hardly taking a day off, not even Christmas.

Agassi had money. He had a place in history. He didn't need this grind. But if Agassi had been content with a career that was, if he had given up on his resurrection, he wouldn't have been able to capitalize on his enduring fame for the sake of charity.

Would there have been millions raised for AIDS research at his annual benefits or a charter school built in his name for forgotten children in Las Vegas? "It does make you wonder," Agassi once said in an interview. "You look at what tennis created. My commitment would have been the same, but the results would have been different."

Agassi needed Reyes and a support group that ultimately included his wife, Steffi Graf, to create a revival that changed everything.

Who does Serena need? She has a talent edge — one far greater than Agassi ever had on his competition — but what is the fitness of her will?

"She has to do this herself," Price said. "Everything has to come from her."

The choice is hers: Does she ask for help? Does she need it? If she is anything like Andre — and so many parallels are there — she does.

Williams Could Use an Etiquette Lesson

BY SELENA ROBERTS | SEPT. 5, 2007

IN HER WHITE ball cap, with a tad of strawberry blonde in her ponytail, Justine Henin has always channeled a little Peppermint Patty — a bit rough around the edges, never completely hip to social graces.

Serena Williams must have thought Henin rude last night. Under the lights Williams craves, in front of an adoring audience inside Arthur Ashe Stadium, Henin snipped the strings on the Tour's most famous parachutist.

To the end of her quarterfinal victory, Henin displayed snappy footwork fit for "Riverdance," gaining aggression as the match wore on. At the end of an exhausting first-set tie breaker, Williams's feet began hitting the hard court heavy and flat while she sprayed forehands on critical points.

"I think she made a lot of lucky shots," Williams said of Henin's play.

All 30 winners were bits of fortune? Who is classless now?

The grumpy, borderline caustic disposition of Williams after her 7-6 (3), 6-1 loss was a little jarring considering she had her own lack of preparation to blame for giving in so easily to Henin.

Did her lack of match play affect her? What about her suspicious fitness?

"I'm very fit," she said. "I can run for hours."

She didn't make it two hours against Henin. What Henin proved is that Williams cannot just drop in on the Tour, anymore, with tennis cameos in between sitcom cameos, in between commercial cameos. Williams cannot just materialize with a pedestrian's lung capacity and swoop in for a major as she did at the Australian Open.

Maybe that wasn't a trend, but an aberration.

Henin wasn't in Melbourne this year during her divorce. If she had been on the scene, Henin might have ended Williams's assault just as she cut short Williams's runs at the French Open and Wimbledon this year.

Instead, Williams's Aussie revival emboldened her, validating her piecemeal approach to tennis. Now, Henin has to have given Serena pause about that strategy. Now, the Open hopes for the Williams family have been cut in half, with a potential Venus-Serena semifinal foiled by Henin.

Henin saved everyone from that sister-sister awkwardness — even the Williams family.

"I think it's better to lose to someone else than your sister," Oracene Price, Serena's mother, said last night.

If Venus gets past her quarterfinal today, Henin would have to beat another Williams to gain a final date in prime time. If Venus plays with the ferocity of her first week, she'll be there to greet Henin, who pushed Serena all over the court by sneaking in for sharp volleys and coming up with a surprise ace or two.

"I've been aggressive, like the No. 1 player in the world, you know, trying to dictate points," Henin, the top Open seed, said. "I'm very happy to beat Serena here in this stadium, in a great atmosphere."

The crowd saw a different Henin. She has used the past few months to reintroduce herself to the public after her personal makeover: inside, not out.

Not long ago, Henin was abrasive, almost cold. In awkward moments in her career, Henin ignored etiquette. She has often been too consumed by intensity, too naked in her ambition to play Miss Manners.

She was guilty of a tennis taboo when she pulled out of the 2006 Australian Open final — after dropping the first set — with stomach pains. And at the 2003 French Open semifinal, Henin put up a hand to call for time on the serve of her opponent, who happened to be Serena. The umpire never saw Henin's signal. And Henin never confessed.

Henin's act of mischief — or, as Serena called it at the time, "lying and fabricating" — was not an oddity. Henin has been known to look to her box to pick up what look to some to be covert signs from her coach.

She still does that. But her edges have been rounded. To all those dying to love Henin, to the purist who treasures her poetic one-handed backhand, and to anyone who digs wispy underdogs in a sport overtaken by power, Henin has become more embraceable.

Maybe it's a product of her recent divorce or reconciliation with her family, but Henin is working toward rehabbing her image.

The stadium crowd pulled for Williams, but they couldn't help but be awed by Henin's guile on points, by her perseverance during rallies. She wasn't the glamorous one or famous one or the babbling one who says whatever runs through her mind.

Henin is not the loquacious and absent-minded Serena, who, from one question to the next, just lets her thoughts fly like daffodil seeds. "I can't keep up with what I say on a daily basis," Serena said this week when asked about a particular response she couldn't remember. "I might have been just jabbering at my lips. Might have just been filling space."

She filled in no blanks last night. Serena barely said a word, bitter and belligerent and discourteous. Who could use charm school now?

Serena Williams Isn't Able to Defend Her Title

BY CHRISTOPHER CLAREY | JAN. 22, 2008

MELBOURNE, AUSTRALIA — Serena Williams, a surprise winner at the Australian Open last year as an unseeded outsider, was a surprise loser Tuesday against Jelena Jankovic in the quarterfinals. Williams's fine, early form in this tournament dissolved in a sea of unforced errors, halting steps and oddly unconvincing serves.

Seeded seventh, Williams had her serve broken seven times as the third-seeded Jankovic won, 6-3, 6-4, in 1 hour 39 minutes to reach her first semifinal in Melbourne. She will face the winner of Tuesday's late match between No. 1 Justine Henin and No. 5 Maria Sharapova.

"It's amazing to beat the defending champion and in general a champion like Serena," Jankovic said. "It doesn't happen every day. I'm happy to get another win against her."

The emotive, extroverted Jankovic now holds a 3-2 edge over Williams, but lost to her in last year's Australian Open in a lopsided, straight-set defeat in the fourth round.

"Now getting revenge, it feels so good," Jankovic said.

Jankovic, 22, had to save three match points against Tamira Paszek of Austria in a first-round match that she won, 12-10, in the third set.

"When I think about, I get goose bumps actually," she said. "When you see the match point I saved on that first day, you wouldn't believe I could actually win that point when it started.

"Being in a semifinal after those matches where I survived, it doesn't get better than that."

Jankovic had nasal surgery in the off-season, which she said has helped to improve her breathing. But she has had a series of minor injuries in the early season, putting herself through ice baths for therapy and taking anti-inflammatory medication.

"I cannot give you all the details, because if I would begin I would never stop," Jankovic said. "I don't have big injuries, but I have pains and soreness in many places."

Leading 3-2 in the second set Tuesday, she was treated for a left quadricep injury, a changeover during which Williams was also treated for a blister on the big toe of her right foot.

"I'm like a wounded animal but I still keep going," Jankovic said. "But the most important thing is I fight on the court and always give my best and never give up."

Williams, who broke a racket in anger on court after losing her serve to go down 1-3 in the second set, was not immediately available for comment, announcing that she would speak with the news media after her women's doubles quarterfinal later Tuesday. She and her sister Venus were scheduled to face the strong Chinese team of Yan Zi and Zheng Jie.

Asked if Serena Williams's performance against Jankovic was linked to an injury or some other physical problem, Oracene Price, her mother and coach, responded: "I'm not going to say, you've got to talk to her. I'm not going to say anything, because Jelena did a great job."

Though this match sometimes had an edge, Price and Jankovic's mother, Snezana, were chatting merrily in the players' lounge shortly after the match.

Williams won here in 2003, 2005 and 2007 but has now lost in the quarterfinals in her last four Grand Slam tournaments. She arrived in Australia trimmer than a year ago and had played often dominant tennis in the early going in Melbourne, beating two powerful teenagers, Victoria Azarenka and Nicole Vaidisova, with relative ease in the last two rounds.

Jankovic's two-handed backhand is her best shot, and she hurt Williams with it consistently. She also took advantage of Williams's mediocre serving: winning 75 percent of the points when Williams put her second serve in play.

On the men's side, Lleyton Hewitt scuffed and scampered around the new surface for which he had lobbied making one wonder how much more blue-painted ground he might have covered or how many more returns and lunging ground strokes he might have put back into play if he had not been forced to go to bed when Melbourne was waking up Sunday.

"Of course he was tired and exhausted," Novak Djokovic said after his 7-5, 6-3, 6-3 victory in the fourth round had put an end to the latest of Hewitt's increasingly unlikely attempts to win his home Grand Slam event.

Hewitt declined to blame the loss on the strange-but-true fact that his previous match against Marcos Baghdatis had set a dubious standard by not starting until shortly before midnight and not finishing until 4:34 a.m.

"Absolutely not; he was too good tonight," Hewitt said of the third-seeded Djokovic.

Changes will presumably be made in the future here to avoid such bleary-eyed shenanigans. It was surely no coincidence that Monday's match between Djokovic and Hewitt led off the night session at the much more reasonable hour of 7:30 and was the only singles match on the schedule. But the fans, including the Australian actress Nicole Kidman, did not get a marathon for their money (or complimentary celebrity pass).

Djokovic has yet to drop a set in four matches, which is not the case for the top-seeded Roger Federer, who lost two in the third round before prevailing against Djokovic's inspired Serbian countryman Janko Tipsarevic.

Federer should have lost another against Tomas Berdych, a Czech player who ruined Federer's Olympics in Athens in 2004 by upsetting him but has since misplaced the keys to the fortress. Berdych had two set points in the second-set tie breaker this time but failed to seize either opportunity, dumping a forehand drop shot into the bottom of the net at 6-5 and then missing another short forehand at 7-6.

He ended up losing the set on another forehand error and was not the same again as Federer advanced to the quarterfinals, 6-4, 7-6 (7), 6-3.

Federer will now face James Blake, a thoughtful, huge-hitting American, who has been nothing but his foil in their previous seven matches. Blake, seeded 12th, is riding high after helping the United States win the Davis Cup in December.

Blake, at first, seemed much more excited about his beloved Giants reaching the Super Bowl than his first quarterfinal at the Australian Open. But he eventually got around to talking about Federer, who has looked vulnerable at times here.

"I'm not going to think too much about that or think that it's going to be any easier," Blake said.

Venus Williams reached the quarterfinals with a 6-4, 6-4 victory against Marta Domachowska, a big-hitting qualifier from Poland. On Wednesday, Williams will play fourth-seeded Ana Ivanovic, the bigger hitter who has trimmed down and improved her serve.

Making Tennis the Top Priority Brings Serena Williams the No. 1 Ranking

BY KATIE THOMAS | SEPT. 8, 2008

SERENA WILLIAMS WAS explaining how her United States Open championship on Sunday was due to a newfound balance between tennis and life when she stopped in midsentence and smacked her forehead.

"Oh, God!" she said. "I have to turn in some designs tomorrow!"

The sketches, she explained to a handful of reporters in a roundtable interview Monday, were due on Tuesday to her fashion line, Aneres.

"I have to turn in some dresses and stuff, and they're going to be rather disappointed," she said. "I'm just going to do like I always did when I was in school. I'm going to do it all tonight."

Procrastination is not new for Williams, of course. Beginning in 2004, when she lost to Maria Sharapova in the final at Wimbledon, critics accused her of showing up unprepared for tournaments. Since then, she has faced consistent questions about whether her off-the-court life — her fashion line, an acting career, even the murder of her half-sister in 2003 — was getting in the way of her tennis.

Now, it seems, tennis is once again at the top of the list.

Williams appeared relaxed during the 20-minute interview Monday as she curled herself into a leather armchair at a Midtown restaurant and tucked her feet, clad in a pair of gold ballet flats, beneath her powerful legs. She had spent the morning making appearances on the "Today" show and "Live with Regis and Kelly," and posing with her trophy in Times Square.

Not only had she won the United States Open, but the first-place finish also bestowed the honor of being the world No. 1 in women's tennis, her first time at No. 1 since August 2003. Back then, she held the position for 57 weeks. This time, she said, she hopes to repeat the feat.

"I feel like I don't want to be No. 1 unless I can stay No. 1," Williams said. "So you know, I'm definitely going to put in the effort to stay there."

But she acknowledged that doing so would not be easy. After Justine Henin retired in May, the top women's ranking has changed hands several times, and no fewer than six players had a chance to claim the spot when the Open began two weeks ago.

"I will probably have to play a little more," Williams said.

She dismissed questions about whether she let other interests get in the way of tennis in recent years. In 2006, she fell outside the top 125 and there were questions of whether she was squandering her world-class talent. Williams, however, said knee surgery in 2003 had a lot to do with the lull in her game.

"I definitely don't think I got complacent," she said. "No excuse, but I had major surgery."

Still, she acknowledged that in recent months she had put more of a priority on tennis, learning how to pursue an ambitious career while finding time for other interests.

"I know it can be done, you just have to put the effort behind it," she said. "You have to train and do everything you do and then have fun, you know? So before, I didn't know how to balance as much, but now I'm good at it."

Williams also attributed her success to a new, and perhaps counterintuitive, mental strategy — learning to relax whenever she is behind.

"In the past I'd get a little nervous, a little tight, and you know really go for it," she said. "I think that worked as well, too. But just these two weeks, I just got so relaxed when I was down, I felt like I had nothing to lose."

Whatever the tactic, it appeared to be working. Williams did not drop a set during the two-week tournament. In the quarterfinal match against her sister Venus, she said she told herself jokes whenever she was down.

"I was standing, she was serving, and I was like, Come on, you better start moving your feet or you're going to be in the third set," she said. "And I would start laughing to myself and I just got relaxed."

Returning to the Top, but With a New View

BY BEN ROTHENBERG | OCT. 26, 2012

ISTANBUL — Serena Williams has hit a ball across a net more times than anyone could ever count, in settings ranging from nighttime finals at the Australian Open to early morning childhood practice sessions in Florida.

Mary Pierce, the retired two-time Grand Slam champion, said this week, recounting her days in Delray Beach, Fla., in the early 1990s: "I was living in an apartment on the third floor, and right below me were some clay courts. And I'm telling you, I don't know how many mornings I would hear the ball being hit. And I was like, Who are these people playing in the morning?

"They'd wake me up, and I'd look out my window, and there they are: the Williams family. And they were all on the court. They were on the court all day long, from morning until night. They would sit on the court and eat lunch. All day, hitting balls and hitting balls and hitting balls."

Two decades later, Williams can still hit those tennis balls better than any woman.

"Whenever Serena is healthy and fit and wants it, she's tops," Pierce said.

Those factors have not always been properly aligned into a winning constellation for Williams, but they are in 2012.

Williams, 31, won Wimbledon and the United States Open this summer, her 14th and 15th Grand Slam singles titles. She also added gold medals in singles and doubles at the London Olympics, and three other WTA singles titles.

Still, she sits at No. 3 in the WTA rankings, a status that will not improve even if she goes on to win this week's WTA Championships. Williams reached the semifinals with a 3-0 record in round-robin play, not dropping a set. The most emphatic win was a 6-4, 6-4 dispatching of top-ranked Victoria Azarenka of Belarus, whom she beat in the United States Open final and three other times this season.

Heading into Saturday's match against No. 4 Agnieszka Radwanska, Williams has compiled a 56-4 record in 2012 — a comparable record to her 56-5 mark in 2002, when she won three Grand Slam events.

"I feel like back then I was really just cruising and on the rise," Williams said. "Now it's a different scenario because I've been through so much in my life. I've had triumphs, disasters, happy moments, and I've had sad moments.

"I think when your career comes complete circle like that, you can really appreciate every win more and more."

It is not just tennis — she has played at least one event each month this year — that has filled Williams's schedule.

After winning a tournament in Charleston, S.C., in April, Williams boarded a plane to Tampa, Fla., to appear on the Home Shopping Network, where she sold her line of leggings and tops. She has had three stints on the network this year; she does four live two-hour blocks in a day.

"It's a lot harder than playing tennis, that's for sure," Williams said. "But it's my job, it's also what I do, and I enjoy it. And I do it, and I love it. I can't sit still; I have to move. If I finish one thing, I'm on to the next, then if I finish that, I'm on to the next. For me it's back-to-back-to-back."

The Frenchman Patrick Mouratoglou has coached Williams since shortly after her shocking loss in the first round at the French Open in May.

"I think it's difficult for us and for other players to understand how difficult it is to keep the motivation when you've won so much, so many tournaments, so many Grand Slams, and been so many times No. 1," Mouratoglou said. "It's not easy."

He added: "Also with her is difficult, because sometimes she played and won Grand Slams being out of shape, in her career. So it's always the same problems with the talented players, because they can win without preparing."

Williams said of her recent relocation to Paris, the site of Mouratoglou's academy: "When you've been playing professional for 15 years, you need a change sometimes. It's almost like I'm starting over. When you first come out on tour, you have so much excitement and you're so hungry because everything is kind of new. I feel like it's all coming back like that for me."

Although her partnership with Mouratoglou largely inspired the move, he emphasized that it was crucial for Williams to stay connected to her roots, to the time of those early morning practice sessions in Florida that woke up Pierce.

"I think that's one of her big strengths, that she has a special mentality," Mouratoglou said. "And that's why it's so important that she stays in touch with her parents and her family, because that's where she got this spirit from."

CHAPTER 3

Professional Maturity and Competing as a Mother

When Serena Williams reached age 30, some questioned how long she could endure as a top competitor. Many of her peers had retired, but Williams continued to win Grand Slam titles. However, her pregnancy and resultant break from tennis at 35 increased this uncertainty, despite having won the Australian Open while eight weeks pregnant. Williams returned to tennis in early 2018, and though she initially struggled and had the added disadvantage of competing as an unseeded player, her detractors were again proven wrong as Williams made her way into the 2018 Wimbledon finals.

Surprising Even Herself, Williams Rallies to Title

BY CHRISTOPHER CLAREY | SEPT. 9, 2012

AFTER A SET, a fourth United States Open title for Serena Williams looked like a foregone conclusion as she ripped serves and ground strokes Sunday at Arthur Ashe with the same intimidating blend of power and precision that has defined her summer.

Who could have imagined then that by the end of this fine, tornado-free evening, victory would come as a surprise, leaving Williams with her eyes wide and her hands to her head?

"I was preparing my runners-up speech," Williams said.

She would have been obliged to deliver it if the world's No. 1-ranked player, Victoria Azarenka, had seized her opportunity when serving for the match at 5-4 in the third set. Although Azarenka had done an often-admirable job of coping with Williams's first-strike pressure in this big-swinging final, she could not quite handle the chance to win her first United States Open.

She lost the first three points, two with unforced backhand errors, and then soon lost the game with a forehand in the tape. Williams, whose form and body language had fluctuated wildly after the opening set, would not lose her way again, putting an exclamation point on the feel-good story of her summer of tennis by closing out a 6-2, 2-6, 7-5 victory that will rank among her most memorable.

In May, Williams made personal history of a more painful sort when she lost in the first round of a Grand Slam tournament in singles for the first time, losing her nerve and her rhythm against Virginie Razzano of France on clay at the French Open.

"I have never been so miserable after a loss," said Williams, who responded by training in Paris under a new coach, Patrick Mouratoglou.

She added: "Sometimes they say it's good to lose. I still would have preferred to win, but, you know, that was forever ago."

So it must seem. Since Paris, Williams, 30, has won the singles and women's doubles at Wimbledon, won the singles and doubles gold medals at the Summer Olympics and now changed her luck at the United States Open, the tournament where she won her first Grand Slam singles title in 1999 at age 17 but where she has lost her temper and the big matches in recent years.

"Now she's starting to really play up to her potential, which is really great to see," said Billie Jean King, the former American women's star, who has counseled Williams. "I think she's very appreciative of her good health now with what she went through and also what her sister is going though. And she is maturing as a person, and you start to appreciate things in a different way as you grow."

There was much to savor Sunday. Her victory over Azarenka, the 23-year-old from Belarus, gave Williams a 15th Grand Slam singles title. Although Azarenka will remain No. 1 and Williams No. 4 on Monday, her victory made Williams the clear player of the year as the only woman to win two major singles titles (three if you consider the Olympics a major).

"Even though I'm 30, I feel so young," Williams said. "I've never felt as fit and more excited and more hungry."

She prevailed despite a significant dip in form in a final in which she hit 44 winners but also made 45 unforced errors. In her first six matches in New York, Williams often looked unbeatable, never coming close to dropping a set. She had not dropped a set in her three previous matches against Azarenka this year, taking a 9-1 lead in their series. At Wimbledon, after she defeated Azarenka, 6-3, 7-6 (6) in the semifinals, Azarenka's coach Sam Sumyk seemed both impressed and perplexed as he talked about the challenge. "It's the power; Vika just didn't have an answer for the power," Sumyk said.

She had no answer in the first set here either as Williams put 64 percent of her first serves into play, dominated the exchanges and won 30 points to Azarenka's 18. But Williams lost her serve in the opening game of the second set on a double fault. When she missed a return as Azarenka took a 2-0 lead, Williams shouted and banged the strings of her racket with her hand.

It was the sound of a champion exiting the zone, and she soon had to deal with a flashback. In her next service game, she was called for a foot fault on a serve on the same baseline where she had been called for a foot fault against Kim Clijsters in the semifinals of the 2009 United States Open. That prompted one of the most infamous tirades in tennis history as Williams threatened and cursed at the lineswoman and was eventually given a point penalty, awarding match point to Clijsters.

CHANG W. LEE/THE NEW YORK TIMES

After dominating the opening set, Serena Williams lost the second. "I was preparing my runners-up speech," Williams said.

This time, Williams held her tongue, but after holding serve to get back to 1-2, she did turn toward the male linesman behind the rose-colored glasses who had called the foot fault and gave him a long, hard stare as she walked to her chair.

"This is the first year in a long time I haven't lost my cool," said Williams, who also lost her temper with the chair umpire in last year's loss in the final here to Samantha Stosur after being penalized a point for hindering Stosur while shouting during an exchange.

But while Williams did not implode Sunday, she did lose command as Azarenka won four of the next five games to even the match at one set apiece. Williams, looking as tight as her strings, struggled to find a balanced platform from which to launch her huge strokes.

Azarenka deserved some of the credit. Hardcourts are her best canvas. She won her first Grand Slam singles title in January at the Australian Open on a similar surface, and she sharpened her game here by surviving a much tougher draw than Williams, defeating Stosur in a three-set quarterfinal and beating the former No. 1 Maria Sharapova in a three-set semifinal.

Azarenka, who has the reach that goes with being six feet tall, is one of the game's best returners. She broke Williams four times and won 59 percent of the second-serve points. But she is also a ferocious baseliner who is remarkably effective at countering big returns off her own serve. As this final developed from a rout into a classic, she repeatedly conjured fast-twitch, quick-swinging half volleys from the baseline.

And yet after 2 hours 18 minutes, it was Williams who ended up leaping and dancing with delight, and Azarenka who ended up in tears in her chair.

"It could have gone my way, probably yes, but it didn't," Azarenka said. "And it really, really hurts, and those emotions come out and you feel sad, but it's time to realize what happened today. You know, it was a great match. It was close but not for me."

Dominant in Her Era, Serena Still Has Time to Build on Legacy

BY CHRISTOPHER CLAREY | SEPT. 10, 2012

IN SEARCH OF the appropriate karaoke song for her latest after-midnight Grand Slam victory party, Serena Williams settled on "I Will Survive."

"I really, really felt those words," Williams said a few hours later as she spoke with a small group of reporters in Midtown on Monday afternoon.

She arrived looking even more imposing than usual in a form-fitting white dress, abundant jewelry and a pair of Christian Louboutin stilettos that pushed the 5-foot-9 Williams well above 6 feet.

But then, why shouldn't she be walking particularly tall at this stage of her career? Traditional rivals like Martina Hingis, Lindsay Davenport, Amélie Mauresmo, Justine Henin and now Kim Clijsters have faded and retired. Her good friend Andy Roddick, the biggest American men's star and a fellow 30-year-old, just played his final tournament, too.

"I've seen too many people retire in my career," Williams said. Yet she survives and, more surprisingly, thrives. The comeback has become such a tennis plot staple that it verges on cliché. But Williams, one of the most ferocious competitors in tennis's lengthy history, has elevated the comeback to a higher art form: a tribute to her enduring drive and enduring edge in power in a sport where other champions have been caught from behind, but where she just won her 15th Grand Slam singles title.

"I don't feel like it's bonus time," she said of victory. "I feel like it's time I deserve to have what I missed."

Last year, she was fearing for her life as she had emergency treatment for blood clots in her lungs. This year, she has put together one of her finest seasons: compiling a 53-4 record and winning Wimbledon, two Olympic gold medals and, on Sunday, the United States Open with an error-filled, winner-filled, drama-filled victory over Victoria Azarenka that might have been the best theater of all of Williams's 15 victories in Grand Slam singles finals.

Williams quibbled with that, putting her three-set win over her sister Venus at the 2003 Australian Open at the top of the list.

But Sunday's match was no family affair with all its attendant mixed emotions. It was full-throated, fully focused combat. Even though Williams has had more symbolic victories in her career, including the 2007 Australian Open with a world ranking of No. 82 or even Wimbledon this year, this triumph had plenty of full-circle qualities, too.

New York was the city where she broke through at age 17 to win her first major singles title. It is also the city where her temperamental outbursts over officials' calls in 2009 and 2011 have deepened the ambivalence she has long generated amid American and global audiences. Even before then, she was a divisive figure, perhaps because, for all her vulnerability off court, she has long projected so little of it between the lines.

But there was no doubt which player the crowd was pulling for Sunday night, and Williams, for a change at Flushing Meadows, did not endanger that good will by losing her cool.

"It's been a love and then hate, hate, hate, hate, hate relationship," Williams said. "It was good to get back yesterday. I don't feel completely comfortable still. You never know what's going to happen, but I do feel much better about the place. I love the crowd. Especially last year, the crowd was so supportive and this year was incredibly supportive. I loved that. But the officials."

She is unquestionably the greatest player of her generation, just as her father, Richard Williams, once suspected she would be despite the talent and achievements of her older sister Venus, who won the last of her seven major singles titles in 2008 at Wimbledon.

But Serena Williams, like Roger Federer before her, is in strong position to encroach on previous generations and is now the first woman in the Open era to have won a Grand Slam singles title 13 years after winning her first.

"She should be the best ever. Why not?" said Billie Jean King, who won 12 major singles titles from 1967 to 1975 and later mentored Williams on the United States Fed Cup team. "But she's got to stay disciplined and fit. When I was captain of Fed Cup, I had a long talk with her, and I had a similar talk with Martina Navratilova when she was young and said, 'You could be the greatest ever.' Now Serena could be the greatest ever, because every generation should get better. She's on her way, but she's still got a way to go."

Despite King's enthusiasm, Williams, who turns 31 on Sept. 26, will probably not catch Margaret Court, who is first on the career list with 24 Grand Slam singles titles.

Nor does she have much chance of reeling in Steffi Graf, who is second with 22 titles.

But third place on the honor roll certainly looks in range if Williams can keep her momentum in the next two seasons. Helen Wills Moody is third, with 19, followed by Martina Navratilova and Chris Evert with 18 and then Williams with 15.

"Well done," Navratilova said to Williams on Twitter on Sunday. "What a gutsy comeback in the third set, you are catching me and Chris, and I don't like it."

That was followed by the frowning-face icon, but Williams grinned when she heard about it.

"It's very motivating," she said of the historical chase. "Since I plan on playing for a long time, definitely plausible. I have to make sure I stay healthy, positive and calm. If I never win another Grand Slam, then I've had a fabulous career and a historic career, and I've done some major things. So I'm really excited either way."

For now, she has a new and excited coach in her corner: the Frenchman Patrick Mouratoglou who in June was still dreaming of working with a Grand Slam champion but now has two major titles and two gold medals on his résumé after serving as a consultant for Williams at Wimbledon, the Olympics and the Open.

She has yet to lose a match with him in her players box. Their connection, at least from Williams's perspective, was happenstance. She was in Paris in May, depressed after losing in the first round of the French Open.

Mouratoglou was an acquaintance, and when she called him to ask if he could send her a practice partner, he invited her to his academy in the suburbs instead.

"I was playing really, really well before him; I mean excellent, but I also love Paris," she said of Mouratoglou. "And I needed a place to train, and it was like, 'Where can I go?' And it works out great because it's a great facility to train at. I love to dance, and he fixed up a studio I can dance in, and once he did that, I knew we were going to be friends for life."

The change of rhythm and routine clearly have played a role in her just-about-all-conquering summer, in which her only loss came in Ohio against German player Angelique Kerber. Though Williams will play exhibitions this year, she plans to play only two more tournaments: the Tier One event in Beijing and the year-end tour championship in Istanbul.

Though she remains only No. 4 in the rankings, in part because of her limited playing schedule and that first-round loss in Paris, there can be no doubt about who has been No. 1 of late.

Serena Williams Will Soon Be 35. But Will She Ever Be No. 1 Again?

BY CHRISTOPHER CLAREY | SEPT. 9, 2016

ANOTHER UNITED STATES Open semifinal had just gone awry for Serena Williams, and Williams's agent, Jill Smoller, and half sister, Isha Price, were in the corridor inside Arthur Ashe Stadium, leaning against a wall and thumbing their smartphones, oblivious to the fact that they were leaning against a huge photograph of Steffi Graf.

Graf, the long-retired German champion, continues to loom large in the age of Serena Williams. And though Williams still has every chance of breaking her tie with Graf and winning an Open-era record 23rd Grand Slam singles title, she now has no realistic chance of breaking her deadlock with Graf for consecutive weeks at No. 1.

At full force, Williams can still be irresistible, as she proved by winning Wimbledon again in July.

But Williams, who will turn 35 this month, is having increasing trouble with the young this season. The 22-year-old Garbiñe Muguruza of Spain beat her to win the French Open. The 21-year-old Elina Svitolina of Ukraine beat her in the third round of the Olympics, and now Karolina Pliskova, 24, of the Czech Republic, has beaten her for the first time, a 6-2, 7-6 (5) upset in their semifinal on Thursday at the United States Open.

"It's getting more and more interesting," said Piotr Wozniacki, the father and coach of Caroline Wozniacki, the Danish star who lost by 6-4, 6-3 to Angelique Kerber in Thursday night's less surprising semifinal. "The new generation is rising up."

In the final Saturday, Pliskova will face Kerber, who beat Williams in the Australian Open final in January, and, at age 28, actually will be the oldest woman in the history of the Women's Tennis Association rankings to make her first appearance at No. 1. She will also be the first German woman since Graf to play in a U.S. Open final.

CHANG W. LEE/THE NEW YORK TIMES

Serena Williams on the court after her straight-sets loss to Karolina Pliskova at the United States Open.

Williams is hardly finished but for now can only watch and consider her accumulating setbacks. In 2015, she was stunned by Roberta Vinci in the semifinals of the U.S. Open, and then decided to end her season and let her body and psyche heal. If she plays on this fall, no certainty in light of injury concerns in recent weeks, she is quite capable of reclaiming the top spot.

Yet there is no doubt that this has been a downbeat year by her standards. She has won only two singles titles, one of them at Wimbledon, and also failed to win a medal at the Rio Olympics last month.

"I mean this year was not good enough," said her coach, Patrick Mouratoglou. "Only one Slam. For Serena, it's not enough, for sure."

Her career, improbable to begin with, has been full of unexpected twists and abrupt shifts in fortune. Thursday's semifinal respected that tradition. After playing one of her better and grittier matches of the year on Wednesday night to beat Simona Halep in three sets,

Williams appeared to have laid the groundwork for a fine stretch run at the U.S.T.A. Billie Jean King National Tennis Center.

Instead, she got overwhelmed by Pliskova in the first set and then failed to fling open the door to a comeback after she had forced it ajar late in the second set.

Down by 0-3 in the tiebreaker, Williams won four straight points, the fourth after a tremendous scrambling get and lob that rebooted a rally which she soon ended with a backhand winner.

It was the sort of spectacular, emotional point that has often shifted momentum in Williams's direction for good. But on the very next point, Williams missed a big first serve by a great distance and then double-faulted.

The magic and the momentum were gone.

Pliskova's coach Jiri Vanek, a former top 100 men's player from Czechoslovakia who was in an understandably giddy mood after the upset, said he was urging her to do "something stupid" to celebrate.

"I said, 'You just beat Serena; you are in the final!' " Vanek recounted on Thursday night in his delightfully imperfect English. "And she's like, 'Let me be me. Go away!' And I said, 'No, come on! Let's go make some funny!' And she was like, 'No, no, no. Be quiet, and let me be.' She's happy with her phone. You know the young."

Williams, who has sometimes faltered in Grand Slam tournaments when obliged to play on consecutive days, as was the case this week, said she was not fatigued after her intense three-set victory over Halep.

"I'm a professional player, been playing for over 20 years," she said. "If I can't turn around after 24 hours and play again then I shouldn't be on tour."

She did, however, make it clear when pressed that she was not 100 percent.

"I have been having some serious left knee problems," said Williams, whose biggest concern coming into the Open was a right shoulder injury that had hampered her serving at the Olympics.

Mouratoglou said that she struck the ground with her left knee in the second round and that the knee got "worse and worse" as the tournament progressed.

"Yesterday with the long match against Halep, it went to another level," he said Thursday.

Though diminished and erratic, Williams was hardly incapacitated. She had that great get in the tiebreaker and her average serve speed was 108 miles per hour, the same as it was against Halep.

Williams has played through plenty of angst and nagging pain in her career and prevailed. Pliskova deserves much credit for handling the moment and beating another Williams sister at the U.S. Open. She saved a match point before defeating Venus Williams in the fourth round, and she beat Serena despite the crowd cheering for her errors and even her double faults.

"For the crowd, it's not probably the best that I beat both of them in their country, but for me it's really something special," Pliskova said. "Obviously the match with Venus helped me not only with the game but with the crowd," adding that it was her first match on center court.

Pliskova has also managed to turn her season and career arc around after falling out of the top 10. Recommitted this season, she still cracked under pressure in the second round of Wimbledon, losing to Misaki Doi of Japan. After that disappointment, Pliskova decided to skip the Olympics and focus on training and preparing for the United States hardcourt season. The result: a big title in Cincinnati and potentially a much bigger title in New York.

Vanek said he kept telling her in practice, "You have to play like Serena or like Petra Kvitova, go for the winners, don't wait for long rallies."

But her improved movement and improved core strength and body positioning also have played a role. She is 6 feet 1 inch.

Getting low to the ball has been a problem in the past, and one of the training tools she has used to address the issue is a belt with elastic bands that attach to her lower legs and force her to move with her knees bent.

"She has to go on the court like that and play volleys," said Vanek, bending down in the U.S. Open players' garden to demonstrate. "And she's screaming, 'I need a chair.'"

Bent knees or not, as Pliskova coolly dispatched one of the world's great athletes, she stood very tall. And now it's time to step up to her first Grand Slam final.

Winning While Pregnant: How Athletes Do It

BY RONI CARYN RABIN | APRIL 27, 2017

THE SNAPCHAT IMAGE of Serena Williams's baby bump with the caption "20 weeks" was deleted shortly after it appeared last week, but anyone could do the math: when Ms. Williams won her 23rd Grand Slam singles title at the Australian Open on Jan. 28, she was eight weeks pregnant. And even her coach had no idea.

"It's an amazing feat," said Dr. Laura Riley, director of labor and delivery at Massachusetts General Hospital in Boston. "People should give her credit for who she is, which is an amazing athlete."

Many women are bone-tired at eight weeks of pregnancy, and hunkered over the toilet with morning sickness. Many go to bed early. A woman's body is going through profound changes as a resident alien the size of a kidney bean settles into her uterus and makes him or herself comfortable.

Progesterone — which surges during pregnancy — is blamed for the extreme fatigue many women experience.

Estrogen and growth factors also surge early in pregnancy. The hormonal changes trigger a cascade of physiological changes. By the fifth week of gestation, the pregnant woman's cardiovascular system has begun to change. Her total blood volume will increase by 35 to 45 percent over the course of the nine months — as will the total number of red blood cells.

With each heartbeat, she pumps out more blood, and she breathes faster. The changes also affect the kidneys, meaning more frequent bathroom runs.

Seven to eight weeks in, up to 80 percent of pregnant women have nausea that can be quite severe and occurs day and night ("morning sickness" is a misnomer, doctors say).

So how did Ms. Williams do it?

"I'm sure there were moments she had to push through fatigue. But she had a job to do, she didn't give in, she pulled out all the stops and got the job done," Dr. Riley said. "A lot of women do that. They have to work."

At the TED 2017 Conference in Vancouver this week, Ms. Williams revealed that she learned of her pregnancy before the tournament began.

"I was nervous," she said. "I wasn't sure what to do. Can I play? I had a lot of questions." She continued: "You hear all these stories about people when they're pregnant — they get sick, they get really tired, really stressed out."

"I knew that at that moment, it was important for me to just focus," she said. "I really felt like I didn't have time to deal with any extra emotions — any extra anything." Ms. Williams added: "Pregnant or not, no one knew. Every tournament where I show up, I'm expected to win."

James Pivarnik, a professor of kinesiology at Michigan State University who has studied the effects of exercise on pregnancy, said research on top athletes is limited, but his hypothesis is that elite athletes are more resilient than most people.

"These women are different. They can recover from incredible stresses that they put themselves through on a daily basis for their entire lives," Dr. Pivarnik said. "One of the reasons they can hit a tennis ball really hard is that they can recover. It's the people who can recover who make it to that level."

Dr. Riley said Ms. Williams's timing was impeccable because there is no reason to avoid competing during early pregnancy; the heavy lifting of pregnancy starts later, around 20 weeks. (Ms. Williams, who announced her engagement to Alexis Ohanian, a businessman, in December, has not played a match since the Australian Open, and a spokeswoman said she will not return to the circuit until 2018).

Dr. Riley said: "My first thought when I heard was, 'Oh my goodness, smart woman, your timing was perfect: It's early in pregnancy and there's nothing to do but sit tight and wait and keep your fingers crossed all goes well.' Nothing she did was going to change that — so why not go out and win the Australian Open?"

Dr. Raul Artal, a professor emeritus of obstetrics and women's health at St. Louis University, said some research has suggested that early pregnancy may even offer an endurance advantage to athletes as a result of the increase in oxygen-carrying red blood cells.

Other athletes who have competed while pregnant include the beach volleyball player Kerri Walsh Jennings, who was five weeks pregnant when she won a gold medal in the 2012 London Olympics. The archers Khatuna Lorig and Cornelia Pfohl were pregnant when they won bronze medals for the Soviet Union and Germany in 1992 and 2000, respectively.

Changes that occur midpregnancy, around 20 weeks' gestation, may interfere with competitive sports. Dehydration can trigger uterine contractions. Joints become more flexible and lax, increasing the risk of joint strains and injuries. And a woman's center of gravity changes, affecting balance.

While pregnancy is not the time to start a strenuous exercise program, physicians generally encourage women to remain physically active. Contact sports like ice hockey are discouraged, but the days of advising pregnant women to avoid exercise are gone. Physical activity guidelines are the same for pregnant and nonpregnant women, and those who have been sedentary are encouraged to take up moderate activities like walking.

Regular moderate physical activity can help reduce excessive weight gain during pregnancy and curbs the risk of complications like gestational diabetes and pre-eclampsia.

"Conventional wisdom years and years ago was to tell women, 'you're pregnant, stay off your feet, put your feet up,' " Dr. Riley said. But now, unless there are specific reasons not to exercise, she said, "We encourage it, in moderation."

The 35-year-old Ms. Williams said she plans to return to competitive tennis after her pregnancy.

"I definitely plan on coming back — I'm not done yet," Ms. Williams said at the Vancouver conference. "This is just a new part of my life. My baby is going to be in the stands, hopefully cheering for me and not crying too much."

After 'a Lot of Ups and Downs,' Serena Williams Nears Her Return

BY CHRISTOPHER CLAREY | FEB. 9, 2018

ASHEVILLE, N.C. — We rule out more major moments and tennis titles at our peril. Serena Williams has proved that point many times over as she has returned from illness, injuries and other turmoil to keep winning the big ones.

Coming back at age 36 from pregnancy and a difficult delivery, after more than a year away, is a new challenge, perhaps her biggest.

"Tennis players have come back after pregnancy and succeeded, yes, but not at this age," said her coach, Patrick Mouratoglou. "All the ones who did it were 10 years younger."

But as Williams practiced on Friday, it was clear from courtside that the desire is still there, even if her fitness, lateral movement and timing have quite a ways to go.

"There's been a lot of ups and downs in the practice," Williams said on the eve of the United States' first-round Fed Cup match here against the Netherlands. "I think that's normal for everything that I've gone through. But it also gives me another view. It's almost relaxing for me because I have nothing to prove. Again, just fighting against all odds to be out there, to be competing again."

She last played an official match on Jan. 28, 2017, when she beat her sister Venus Williams to win the Australian Open without dropping a set in the tournament.

Even after Friday's draw, it was unclear whether she would make her comeback here in singles or doubles (or both). She was not in the singles lineup for the opening-day matches on Saturday. Instead, Venus Williams and CoCo Vandeweghe were listed to play for the United States: Williams against Arantxa Rus and Vandeweghe against Richel Hogenkamp.

For now, Serena Williams is scheduled to play only doubles. She and Lauren Davis would be in the final match on Sunday and would probably be meaningless in light of the teams' relative strengths.

"We're going to be like Serena and stay in the moment," Kathy Rinaldi, the United States Fed Cup captain, told me on Friday. "Tomorrow we know Venus and CoCo are playing, and then we'll make a decision each day like we normally do at Fed Cup. We don't plan everything out. Things happen, and we have to see how everyone is playing and everyone is feeling."

Saturday's lineup will come as a surprise to the casual fans who cannot imagine Serena Williams, winner of an Open-era record 23 Grand Slam singles titles, failing to get priority. But it makes sense in this unusual context.

Venus Williams, at No. 8, and Vandeweghe, at No. 17, are the two highest-ranked players on the American team. Both played full and deeply successful seasons in 2017 when Serena was giving birth to her daughter, Alexis Olympia, and marrying Alexis Ohanian. Vandeweghe also was the undefeated leader of the American team that won the Fed Cup in Belarus in November.

For the first time since she was a teenager, Serena Williams has no ranking, which has not gone unnoticed. Erik Poel, the director of the Dutch Tennis Federation, jokingly referred to that strange state of affairs at the official team dinner on Thursday night as he talked about reasons for the heavily underdog Dutch team to be optimistic.

"We were looking, and a certain S. Williams didn't even have a ranking," Poel said, acting as if that certain S. Williams were an unknown player.

Williams, who was sitting nearby, hunched forward in her chair and roared with laughter while Rinaldi reached back and gave Poel a high five.

But everyone at the tables in Asheville and elsewhere knows full well what S. Williams is capable of, and though it is difficult to imagine her getting back to her peak, who truly has the moxie to proclaim that she won't resume being a champion?

"She's coming back because she believes she can win, otherwise she wouldn't be coming back," Mouratoglou said in a telephone interview from France this week. "It's that simple."

Rinaldi was tossing balls and occasional advice to Williams on Friday as Williams exchanged groundstrokes with Vandeweghe during their practice session. Williams crushed certain shots with customary power and precision but mistimed many others, muttering to herself and shadow-stroking between rallies.

She was in a playful mood, dancing as she walked to the baseline and cracking jokes in her chair during breaks and between deep breaths, but she was all business between the lines.

"I'm sure she does want it to go faster," Rinaldi said of the process. "She's got high expectations obviously, and it's tough to manage those in the beginning and be patient with herself. But as you can see, I think that's what makes her so great, too, is that she is tough on herself and has that drive. She wants to be back, wants to be playing and wants to be winning titles, it seems, and absolutely nobody knows how to do that better than she does."

So what is reasonable in terms of expectations? A few months for Williams to get her bearings, drop some more weight and potentially pose a threat at Wimbledon in July? Or something more ambitious?

"I wouldn't be surprised if she steps back into it and does well, to be honest with you," Rinaldi said. "I've seen her this week, and every day she's better and stronger, and the desire is there."

Olympia, now five months old, is here in Asheville with Williams, who experienced complications after giving birth by emergency cesarean section in September. She has said she spent the first six weeks of motherhood in bed. After her wedding in November, Williams resumed training in earnest in December, a few weeks before she played and lost a lucrative exhibition match to Jelena Ostapenko in Abu Dhabi on Dec. 30.

Ostapenko, the reigning French Open champion, kindly stopped hitting many balls to the corners as the match progressed, and Williams looked underwhelmed with her own play.

Skipping last month's Australian Open seemed a sage decision.

"She really started from zero, doing no physical work for months," Mouratoglou said. "After the pregnancy and the complications, at the beginning she could only do 30 minutes of crosscourt hitting. We couldn't call it real training."

Mouratoglou said he planned to join Williams next week in the United States to prepare for the tournament in Indian Wells, Calif., in March. He anticipates her playing a limited schedule in 2018: Indian Wells, Miami, Rome, Madrid, the French Open, Wimbledon, a hardcourt tournament in North America, the United States Open and then, if she qualifies, the WTA Finals in Singapore.

There is also the Fed Cup, for which she needs to make herself available for three ties in the next two and a half years in order to be eligible for the 2020 Summer Olympics in Tokyo.

"She can't do seasons like 2013 or 2014," Mouratoglou said. "In 2013, she won 11 tournaments. That was herculean. She doesn't have the same age, and I'm not sure she even wants that anymore. The focus for her will be on the big moments."

That means the majors, where she is one championship away from tying Margaret Court's record of 24 Grand Slam singles titles.

I asked Williams on Friday if winning No. 25 was the ultimate goal as she returns.

"Right now, my main goal is just to stay in the moment," she said. "It goes unsaid 25 is obviously something that I would love, but I'd hate to limit myself."

Consider that a warning to the rest of the women's tour, where no single player has managed to dominate in Williams's extended absence. And consider it a sign that motherhood and marriage may have altered her perspective but have done nothing to lower her aim.

Tennis Needs Serena Williams Back. But Does She Need to Be Seeded?

BY CHRISTOPHER CLAREY | MAY 28, 2018

PARIS — As ever, Serena Williams is a conversation starter.

She has generated debate inside and outside of tennis since she took her first swings on the pro tour at age 14 at a time when the WTA had banned 14-year-olds from its main circuit.

Now that she has become one of her sport's greatest champions and a new mother, Williams, 36, continues to set the agenda.

Despite her Open-era record of 23 major singles titles, she is unseeded at the French Open, where she is scheduled to play Kristyna Pliskova on Tuesday in her first match at a Grand Slam tournament in 16 months. Williams also was unseeded at the BNP Paribas Open and Miami Open, the only other tournaments she has played in this start-and-stop comeback in 2018 in which her singles record is 2-2.

When other leading players returned from maternity leave, including Kim Clijsters and Victoria Azarenka, there was no uproar when they were not among the seeds. But Williams is not just any leading player, and the women's tour, in the midst of an extensive review of its policies, is now being pressured to change its rules.

Change seems all but certain. It seems likely that players coming back from pregnancy in the future will be able to return with a protected ranking after a longer period than the current two years, and they may be allowed to use that special ranking in more tournaments than the current eight.

But change on the seeding issue is far from certain. The issue is thornier than it might first appear, and reaching consensus among the players is hardly straightforward.

"It is a complex one, and I think it's complex because it's not your normal work environment," said Steve Simon, the chief executive of the WTA Tour, in a telephone interview on Monday. "It is competition.

You're dealing with independent contractors, and by the nature of competition you are not guaranteed anything. But yet there is a feeling you should have some rights, and I think our rules do address a lot of that. It really is just one element of the rule, to be honest, which is in discussion. That's the use of the special ranking for seeding."

Williams, like all WTA players returning from maternity leave, has a protected ranking that she can use to enter eight tournaments in a 12-month period. Williams was No. 1 before she took her break from the game in February 2017.

She and some of her leading rivals, including the current No. 1 Simona Halep, have argued that there should also be protected seedings, both to avoid unbalanced draws and to not dissuade players from having children earlier in their careers.

"You shouldn't have to stop altogether just because you want to have a baby young," Williams told me in a recent interview. "You don't want to be my age having your first baby, you know what I mean? So I think as a women you should have that choice to get pregnant and have a baby and still be able to have a career just like in any other job."

Do you need protected seeding to achieve that in tennis?

"I think you do," Williams said, before referring to Azarenka, a 28-year-old former No. 1 player, who also recently returned to the circuit after childbirth.

"Victoria is doing amazing, she really is, and she's also had a lot of time to get fit and be ready," Williams said. "But some players, they work their whole lives to be top 30 and they start doing really well, decide to have a family, and it takes them a while to get back and to have to do all that work again."

For Williams, it does not seem fair to have to start from scratch with no seeding, and even Ivanka Trump chimed in last week, tweeting, "No person should ever be penalized professionally for having a child. The #WTA should change this rule immediately."

But other players who have recently returned from pregnancy do not see it as starting from scratch and are concerned about those who would be penalized by guaranteeing returning mothers a seeding. Mandy Minella, a 32-year-old from Luxembourg, just made it into the main draw of this French Open with a special ranking of 104 after giving birth to her daughter, Emma, in October.

Like Azarenka, whose special ranking is No. 6, Minella lost in the first round on Monday.

"When you come back, you shouldn't be seeded because you have players who work all year and play good all year to earn the seeding spots," Minella told me. "In a Grand Slam, if you would put in this case Serena as the first seed, the No. 32 is pushed out."

Minella still wants change: she thinks returning mothers should be able to use a special ranking for at least 12 tournaments, not eight. But in Minella's view, she and Williams do have access to the workplace: a spot in the main draw. They just don't deserve automatic access to a privileged position in that workplace, much as a W.N.B.A. player returning from pregnancy is not guaranteed a spot in the starting lineup.

"We want to have Serena Williams," Minella said. "We want to see her. She's important for tennis, and she can be in any tournament. I think if she's fit enough, she will come back to where she belongs, right? But she has to prove herself again after practicing. In sport, you have to prove yourself over and over again."

That would be true with or without a protected seeding. You still have to beat seven players to win a major singles title, and with Williams not having played a competitive clay-court match in nearly two years, that will be quite a challenge in Paris.

This is the most difficult surface for many players to adjust to, Williams included. She already has proved that she can win Wimbledon on grass without playing warm-up events. But she has never won any of her three French Open titles without competing on clay in the lead-up.

Williams's draw here could have been worse: Pliskova is unseeded and has yet to win a French Open match. But Williams could potentially face seeded players in the next six rounds if she were to do the unlikely and reach the final. (It's been done: Clijsters, then 26 and unseeded, won the 2009 United States Open, her third tournament back after taking more than two years off to have her first child.)

French Open officials have been criticized for not including Williams among their 32 seeded women, but Guy Forget, the tournament director, made the very good point that the WTA Tour itself does not allow Williams a seeding under its current rules. Why should Roland Garros do so?

Wimbledon, which has a tradition of deviating from the rankings in its seeding because of the specificity of grass, is likely to take a different approach. Williams is a seven-time Wimbledon singles champion and won the title in 2015 and 2016, her most recent appearances. Even if rusty, she has to be considered one of the 32 biggest grass-court threats in the world.

Azarenka, a member of the WTA Player Council, said it was important to make a rule that would work not just for Williams but for everyone.

"This conversation was not on the table last year when I was coming back, and I was not seeded in Wimbledon," she said. "Wimbledon has the choice to do that, and this year they are going to be seeding Serena."

That is not yet certain, but the WTA Tour once had this discretion, with its chief executive authorized to use a special ranking for seeding purposes at its own events.

Lindsay Davenport was seeded this way at several tournaments in 2002, as were Serena Williams and Venus Williams in 2004 before the rule was changed after pushback from other players.

But Davenport and the Williamses were returning from injury, not pregnancy, in those years. The feeling now is that the injury and pregnancy should be treated differently in the WTA rule book. If there is change, it is likely to have little impact on Williams. Simon said if the rule was revised, it would not be put in place until the start of the 2019 season.

He and Azarenka defended the integrity of the process on Monday.

"It's very easy to say, 'Oh, you know, they are not seeded, it's a terrible, bad rule,' " said Azarenka, who is ranked 84th and has a 11-6 record since returning to tour last June. "But there are a lot of things that are going into this rule and into the thought process. So I would like to just, for the record, say that please give us time and we will, as a women's association, we will make sure that we have the best for women players and for our sport."

Building consensus does seem the right way to go here. So does making the right move for everyone, not just the greatest women's player of this era.

The 'Real Serena' Emerges and Roars Back at the French Open

BY CHRISTOPHER CLAREY | MAY 31, 2018

PARIS — Ash Barty had to know it was coming. After all these years, we all had to know it was coming.

Serena Williams's personal life and priorities have certainly changed in the past 16 months, but she was not going to bid adieu to the French Open without a fight.

Muted and off target as she lost the first set to the 17th-seeded Barty on Thursday night, Williams did not start the next set any more convincingly. Some French members of the crowd began to shout "Allez!" in a manner that was more reproachful than supportive.

She lost her serve at love to open the second set, making three consecutive unforced errors. She then moved forward on the first point of the next game and mishit an overhead off the top of her racket frame, sending the ball flying well past the baseline.

But she abruptly changed the tone of this second-round match, raising her volume and her intensity. Her game soon followed.

By the end, with the light fading, Williams had done what she has done so often on the show courts of the world: rallying — with a vengeance — to win.

Final score: 3-6, 6-3, 6-4.

"I think she's not quite at the level she was when she was at her best, but that's normal; that's expected," said Barty, a 22-year-old Australian. "But her level when she's not quite at her best is still bloody good. And yeah, I think when push came to shove, the real Serena came out."

The increasingly intriguing question in Paris is how often the real Williams will continue to make an appearance as she works her way back after maternity leave.

Rust be damned, she is now into the third round, where she will face another very tricky opponent in Julia Görges, the powerful No. 11

seed from Germany. Get past Görges, and Williams would face either Maria Sharapova or Karolina Pliskova, both former No. 1s.

It is a rough-and-tumble draw.

"Frankly I prefer that she plays matches against dangerous players," said Patrick Mouratoglou, her coach. "That brings out the best in Serena each time. She goes for it more, because she knows she has no choice, so I like when she gets tough draws. It's never kept her from winning a Grand Slam. That's not what's going to stop her."

She has won 23 of them in singles, one short of Margaret Court's record. But Williams has never been in a position quite like this. She arrived at Roland Garros not having played a clay-court tournament in two years and not having played any tournament since losing in a hurry to Naomi Osaka in the first round of the Miami Open on March 21.

Williams has come back before from extended breaks and experienced quick success, but she is now 36 with an infant daughter, Olympia, born last September.

Since returning to competition in February, Williams has played only six singles matches and had not played in a Grand Slam tournament since her run to the Australian Open title in January 2017 when she was two months pregnant.

"I have definitely always had that will to win," Williams said after defeating Barty. "It was something I was born with, thank goodness. This is a Grand Slam. You know, this is my first one back. I want to be able to just do my best and one day tell my daughter that I tried my best. When I was out there, that's all I was just trying to do."

What made that task more complicated on Thursday was the stiffness and soreness she was feeling after playing singles on Tuesday and then doubles on Wednesday with her sister Venus.

"The recovery for a first match is always difficult," said Williams, who was back in the full-length black bodysuit she wore in the first round. "Every year in Australia when I play, the first match is, like, killer no matter how much preparation I do. And the same here, it's killer, but once the adrenaline sets in, it's fine."

Still, the chiaroscuro disparity between Williams in the first set and Williams in the final two sets on Thursday was startling, at least until you consulted your memory bank.

"The emotion, passion and game came back," said Chris Evert, the seven-time French Open champion who is an analyst for Eurosport here. "We've seen this hundreds of times. Serena knows it, and unfortunately for Barty, she knew it, too. It then turns into a psychological battle for Barty."

Technically, this was an upset. Williams is unseeded here, and Barty was actually the bookmakers' consensus favorite, a rarity for any Williams opponent, despite never having defeated a top 50 opponent on clay.

Beating Williams, who is currently ranked 451st, would not have changed that, but it certainly would have been something to tell the grandchildren about around the "barbie" in Australia many years from now.

Barty has a remarkably complete game, and tennis fans (and tennis purists) should be delighted that she ultimately chose to return to the sport after struggling with the expectations in Australia and playing cricket instead for a time.

At 5-foot-5, she is shorter than most leading players, but she generates great leg drive and racket-head speed on her serve and is as comfortable punching away volleys at the net as she is generating topspin or very crisp slice in the backcourt.

What she lacked on Thursday was a more reliable first serve (she put just 55 percent into play) and a more reliable forehand under duress as Williams started to find her range and attack.

"That's what Serena does to you," said Alicia Molik, the Australian Fed Cup captain, who was watching from Barty's player box. "Serena makes you probably go for that extra 1 percent that you normally might not need to try to execute, and sometimes that's just enough to force you to miss."

Still, it was unquestionably a missed opportunity for Barty. Now it will be Görges's turn to see if she can capitalize on Williams's continuing search for top form. They have played only twice, but not since 2011; Williams won both matches.

"The name Williams has incredible status in tennis and rightfully so," Görges, 29, said. "Still, I believe you've got to distance yourself a little from the name of your opponent. I want to play my game, regardless of who is on the other side. Sometimes that is easier said than done, but that is how I want to go about this match."

Görges's game is based on big serving and her big forehand. She has never been past the fourth round in a Grand Slam tournament, but is 22-10 so far in 2018 and one spot away from her career-high ranking of 10.

"That's a tough one for Serena; I honestly wouldn't expect her to win that," said Pat Cash, the former Wimbledon champion who is coaching the American player Coco Vandeweghe. "But it's different when you're out there on center court, and Serena's been there so many times. So you know, she's got a chance. She competes better than anybody for a long, long time. She gets out of matches or wins matches she has no right to win."

In part that is because Williams genuinely relishes a challenge, and she certainly has an epic one on her hands: trying to get back to the top at age 36.

"If I were to play my former self, I'm not sure I would win," she said. "But I can't say I would lose. And thank God I don't have to do that, so it works out great for me."

What is clear is that no one left in the tournament is looking at Williams as an unseeded long-shot anymore. Self-belief is not an issue.

Informed post-match that Novak Djokovic had said she was the "greatest female athlete of all time, probably," Williams responded by saying "probably" and then saying nothing more, looking as if she had just received a backhanded compliment.

Serena Williams and Maria Sharapova to Reboot a Rivalry After Life Intervened

BY CHRISTOPHER CLAREY | JUNE 2, 2018

PARIS — It will be Serena Williams versus Maria Sharapova at a Grand Slam tournament on Monday, but don't think that this will be business as usual.

Despite playing little competitive tennis in the last 16 months, Williams may well win again. Just as she has won her last 18 matches against Sharapova, the only women's player in this era who has rivaled Williams's star power and earning power, yet has never rivaled her as a champion.

But Williams's and Sharapova's lives and perspectives are altered now, and both have something different to prove as they prepare for this fourth-round French Open duel and all that might happen beyond it — for the winner — in Paris this spring.

Williams, who defeated 11th-seeded Julia Görges, 6-3, 6-4, on Saturday in the finest performance of her comeback from maternity leave, wants to show herself and anyone else concerned that she can resume being the game's dominant force as a 36-year-old who gave birth to a daughter, Olympia, just nine months ago.

Sharapova, a two-time French Open champion who routed sixth-seeded Karolina Pliskova, 6-2, 6-1, on Saturday, wants to make it unmistakably clear that she can be every bit as good as she was before a 15-month suspension for a doping violation that began in early 2016.

Without such meaty challenges, it is possible that both would be retired by now. Sharapova, though only 31, has been playing on tour since she was 14 and training in a professional manner since she was a preteenager fighting for her place in the sun at the IMG Tennis Academy in Bradenton, Fla., as her father, Yuri, a Russian immigrant, struggled to make the finances work.

TIM CLAYTON/CORBIS SPORT/GETTY IMAGES

Serena Williams in action against Julia Görges of Germany in the evening light on Court Suzanne Lenglen in the Women's Singles Competition in June 2018.

But Williams's and Sharapova's ambitions and story lines are about to collide again on Monday in the midst of a women's competition that is far more compelling than the men's event here.

With Williams and Sharapova back in the mix in Paris, finding sufficiently grand venues to showcase all the leading women proved challenging in the third round on Saturday. The world No. 1 Simona Halep, a two-time French Open finalist, had to trek all the way out to the new Court 18 in the hinterlands of Roland Garros to face Andrea Petkovic.

Halep prevailed, 7-5, 6-0.

Sloane Stephens, the reigning United States Open champion, also played on Court 18 for her three-set tussle earlier in the day with Camila Giorgi, an Italian who has rarely met a risky shot she was not willing to embrace.

Giorgi served twice for the match in the third set — at 5-4 and again at 6-5 — before Stephens defused the danger.

"She plays kind of crazy, but in a good way," the 10th-seeded Stephens said. "I knew it was going to be a battle, and I just stuck in there and waited for my opportunities."

Angelique Kerber, a former No. 1 and a two-time Grand Slam champion, ended up on Court No. 1 against Kiki Bertens, a major clay-court threat and a French Open semifinalist two years ago. Kerber won, 7-6 (4), 7-6 (4).

"I think for me watching some men's tennis right now, it's like you know who's going to win," said Wim Fissette, Kerber's coach. "A lot of these men's matches, it seems very clear, but the women's game, it's a very exciting period. You cannot tell who's going to win, and you have all these generations coming together."

The women's fourth round in the top half of the draw is now set. It will be Halep against Elise Mertens; Kerber against Caroline Garcia, the last French player left in singles; Garbiñe Muguruza, the 2016 French Open champion, who looks like a woman on a mission, against Lesia Tsurenko; and finally Williams against Sharapova.

That match will be the latest chapter in a would-be rivalry that has never materialized but has seldom lacked a sharp edge.

Sharapova wrote about Williams at length in her recent autobiography, "Unstoppable," an intriguing title in light of how many times Williams has stopped her through the years.

In Sharapova's view, she has never been forgiven for witnessing Williams's tears in the locker room of the All England Club after Sharapova, then just 17, upset her in the 2004 Wimbledon final.

"I think Serena hated me for being the skinny kid who beat her, against all odds, at Wimbledon," Sharapova wrote. "I think she hated me for taking something that she believed belonged to her. I think she hated me for seeing her at her lowest moment. But mostly I think she hated me for hearing her cry."

Williams was asked about that analysis on Saturday night. "I don't have any negative feelings toward her, which was a little disappointing to see in that hearsay book," she said. "Especially having a daughter, I feel like negativity is taught. One of the things I always say: I feel like women, especially, should bring each other up."

Williams also discussed the locker-room incident.

"It's a Wimbledon final, you know, so it's just, like, I think it would be more shocking if I wasn't in tears," she said. "And I am emotional, and I do have emotions, and I wear them on my sleeve. You know, I'm human, so for me, I think it's totally normal. I think what happens there should definitely maybe stay there and not necessarily talk about it in a not-so-positive way in a book."

Bring on the fourth round, which will be Sharapova and Williams's first match since Williams won in the quarterfinals of the 2016 Australian Open, the last tournament Sharapova played before her suspension for using the banned substance meldonium.

"Well, it's been a while," she said of her latest chance to face Williams. "And I think a lot has happened in our lives for the both of us in very different ways."

Sharapova also said: "I think any time you play against Serena you know what you're up against. You know the challenge that is upon you. You know, despite the record that I have against her, I always look forward to coming out on the court and competing against the best player."

Williams is actually unseeded, but both she and Sharapova, the No. 28 seed, are clearly gathering momentum in Paris.

Sharapova, a former No. 1 who worked her way back into the top 30 after returning to the tour in April 2017, was relentless against Pliskova, mixing baseline bolts with deft drop shots. Williams was settled and routinely on target against Görges, a big-serving German who hit 11 aces to Williams's three but who could never get the lead on the scoreboard, struggling to cope with Williams's pace and precision.

Williams's win was quite a performance, all the more so for someone who had not played a clay-court tournament in nearly two years before arriving at Roland Garros.

"Well," said Alexis Ohanian, her husband. "She's always been a trendsetter."

No Storybook Ending for Serena Williams. Instead, a Wimbledon Title for Angelique Kerber.

BY CHRISTOPHER CLAREY | JULY 14, 2018

WIMBLEDON, ENGLAND — The focus has understandably been on Serena Williams's comeback this season.

She was the tennis superstar returning from childbirth with Margaret Court's record of 24 Grand Slam singles titles in her sights.

She was the one showing the way, at age 36, for working mothers and older athletes to keep striving for more.

But Angelique Kerber's comeback has some lessons for the wider world as well: about persistence, about overcoming weaknesses by developing your strengths, and about sticking to your very fine game plan in a Wimbledon final against an opponent of superior power and experience.

Kerber struggled last season after winning two Grand Slam titles in 2016 and moving up to the No. 1 ranking. But at 30, she has made an emphatic return to the top, reaching the semifinals of the Australian Open in January and then winning the trophy she has long wanted most by defeating Williams, 6-3, 6-3, on Saturday.

"No way," said Kerber as she stared at her name on the board of champions inside the clubhouse after the match. "That was always a dream of mine."

Williams has spoken about the delights of playing freely with nothing to lose during her matches at Wimbledon this year, but on Saturday she played and sounded like a champion who was feeling the pressure, some of it self-imposed.

She finished with 24 unforced errors and 23 winners, struggled at the net and failed to dominate with her imposing serve as Kerber broke her four times and lost her own serve just once.

Kerber played a marvelous match. Williams, focused on competing for a greater cause, did not.

"To all the moms out there, I was playing for you today, and I tried," Williams said, tearing up in her post-match interview as the Centre Court crowd cheered to offer its support.

Williams played — and won — the 2017 Australian Open while two months pregnant, but she did not play again on tour until 13 months later. She gave birth to her daughter, Olympia, on Sept. 1, 2017, and suffered complications after her cesarean section, including a pulmonary embolism.

Less than a year later, she was in the final at Wimbledon, which she has won seven times. But she was unable to extend her 20-match winning streak at the All England Club. Her last defeat in singles here was against Alizé Cornet in the third round in 2014.

The women's final began about two hours later than scheduled because of the delayed completion of the men's semifinal between Novak Djokovic and Rafael Nadal, which had been suspended on Friday night. Williams took no issue with the decision to change the timing of the women's final.

"It definitely didn't have an impact on me," she said. "I'm completely a supporter of women and women's sport, obviously. Honestly, I just feel like it was a necessary evil."

And despite her downbeat performance, Williams was upbeat.

"I didn't know a couple of months ago where I was, where I would be, how I would do, how I would be able to come back," she said. "It was such a long way to see light at the end of the road, kind of. So I think these two weeks have really showed me that, O.K., I can compete."

Williams acknowledged she may have come back too soon in March and struggled with her fitness and her timing in her first four matches, losing two of them. She took another two-month break before returning for the French Open in late May, winning three matches before withdrawing with a pectoral injury.

With six more victories at Wimbledon, Williams will rise to 28 in the rankings on Monday, which gives her an excellent chance of being seeded at the United States Open next month without official intervention.

Wimbledon chose to seed her 25th here, although her ranking of 181 made her the lowest-ranked player to reach the singles final.

"I just feel like I'm taking the steps in the right direction," she said. "I took a giant step at Wimbledon, but my journey has just begun."

Kerber grew up watching her role model, Steffi Graf, win Wimbledon on television, including the last of Graf's seven victories here, which came in 1996.

Now, 22 years later, Kerber has given Germany another women's singles champion at Wimbledon and also given her nation a sporting lift.

"After a really embarrassing World Cup, we needed something," said Boris Becker, the former Wimbledon men's champion from Germany, in comments to the BBC.

Kerber, who will rise to No. 4 on Monday, can absorb pace as well as anyone in tennis. She put 87 percent of her returns in play in the tournament and put a remarkable 80 percent in play against Williams, whose other opponents could manage to return less than 60 percent.

With her improved serve, Kerber also held firm in the second set when Williams, true to her past, got tougher, increasing the volume of her grunts and her intensity.

"This is Serena; I know that this is the point she is always doing this, because this is a part of her game," Kerber said.

At 1-1 in the second set on the first point of Kerber's service game, Williams pounded a forehand swing volley straight at Kerber when both were at the net. It sailed long as Kerber avoided it.

"I think Angie reacted well on it," her coach, Wim Fissette, said. "She didn't take it personal or she was not irritated by it, just continued to play her game and focus just on herself."

Kerber made only five unforced errors in the match. But she was also bold when she had to be on the grass that suits her flat strokes and taste for low-bouncing balls.

"I feel Angie started the tournament a bit slow and more with her older game, with just running and fighting," Fissette said. "And after the second round she decided that, 'With this tennis, I'm not going to win. So I have to play my offensive tennis, especially when I need it.' "

Against Williams, she won the first set with her signature shot: a forehand winner down the line. And when Kerber served for the match, Williams threw up a high defensive shot at 30-30 that landed deep, a shot that required Kerber to generate the pace. She did not shrink from the responsibility. She coolly nailed another forehand down the line that landed on the opposite baseline with a puff of chalk for another winner.

When Williams lost the next point, the final point, with a backhand return into the net, Kerber dropped her racket, pitched forward onto her knees and began to cry as she lay on the grass and the dirt.

She and Williams soon met on Kerber's side of the net for an extended embrace.

This is becoming a Grand Slam tradition, this contrast of styles. And Kerber has now won two of their three duels in major finals: defeating Williams in the 2016 Australian Open final, losing to Williams in the 2016 Wimbledon final and winning on Saturday.

Kerber, who also won the United States Open in 2016, owns titles at three of the four Grand Slam events, lacking only the French Open.

Williams has won all four majors at least three times, but, for now, her total remains at 23 — one short of Court's record.

"It's a huge thing for her, coming back after the last few months to being in the final," Kerber said. "For sure she was trying to do everything to beat me today, but I'm sure she will take her next Grand Slam and she will make history for sure."

Fissette, who has now coached five players who have beaten Williams, said he felt her relatively easy draw, in which she faced no seeded players in the first five rounds, might have made it difficult for her to find the necessary gear on Saturday.

"I feel she just missed experience in matches against a really top player who is rock solid, like Angie," Fissette said.

There are no guarantees that No. 24 will come, of course. For all Williams's aura, talent and drive, Kerber is on the rise again and a younger generation is coming. But Williams already has a fine bedtime tale to tell Olympia about a Wimbledon comeback.

"I think it was a happy story," Williams said with a smile. "I'll probably change the ending."

NAILA-JEAN MEYERS contributed reporting.

CHAPTER 4

Venus and Serena: Teammates, Rivals and Sisters

For Serena Williams, following her sister Venus into tennis was both a blessing and a curse. Venus had already established herself as a successful player by the time Serena started, which pressured Serena to measure up to her more experienced sibling. Nonetheless, she also had a doubles partner whom she had played with for years before her professional debut and, perhaps more important, someone to support and commiserate with her through her challenges and victories. Venus and Serena have competed as doubles partners and singles competitors throughout their careers, becoming famous for their "sister act" in the process.

In Williams vs. Williams, Big Sister Moves Ahead

BY ROBIN FINN | JAN. 21, 1998

THEIR BEADS FELL from their Technicolor cornrows and littered the stadium floor. It was proof that meeting your sister in the second round of your first visit to the Australian Open is an unraveling experience, even for the poised and powerful Williams sisters, who have joint designs on the No. 1 ranking now owned by yet another overachieving teen-ager, Martina Hingis.

Today, there were fears that the rank newcomer, 16-year-old Serena, might wreak havoc on the already complicated family pecking order and defeat 17-year-old, 16th-ranked Venus — making good on the prediction by their father, Richard, that the littlest Williams was destined to be the greater champion of the two.

But after a heated beginning in which neither sister gave ground, Serena deferred to her elder and allowed Venus Williams, who made her own Grand Slam breakthrough when she reached the final of the United States Open last summer, to advance into the third round of this one with a 7-6 (7-4), 6-1 victory.

"Serena, I'm sorry I had to take you out," the winner told the loser. "Serena hates to lose, and her reputation is she never loses to any one twice."

Venus is now 2-0 against her less-experienced sibling, and wary of their next encounter, which she hopes will happen in a final.

"I see us as the No. 1 and No. 2 seeds, interchangeable," Venus said.

"Today would have been great fun if it were a final, but it wasn't so fun to eliminate my little sister in the second round."

Serena Williams has made a rankings leap from 304th to the low 40's since announcing herself as the next big threat to the establishment with upsets of Monica Seles and Mary Pierce last November, an upset of second-ranked Lindsay Davenport last week and a significant Grand Slam debut here when she defeated sixth-seeded Irina Spirlea in the opening round.

"If I had to lose in the second round, no better than to Venus; I tried to keep thinking of her as someone else, but I guess Venus has a little more experience than me," said Serena, who tends to be a little more emotional than her older sister.

During the match, which the sisters insisted was an adventure rather than an ordeal, their mother, Brandy, sat in a neutral corner, smiling and fanning herself with her grounds pass.

According to her, it mattered less which sister won the match than how they would treat one another after it was over.

When Serena offered her sister a rather dejected handshake after conceding the match with a netted backhand, Venus immediately put a conciliatory arm around her shoulders and held tight.

Then the two joined hands for a shared bow, evidently the first of many.

"What you saw was something for the future," Serena said.

The sisters were smiling, sort of, and baring their orthodontia a tad uneasily as they met at the net of the sun-dappled stadium court before their first meeting as professionals. The last time the siblings squared off was eight years ago, when Serena, then 8, got all the way to the final of her first junior tournament only to find herself swatted into submission by her big sister, 6-2, 6-2.

Serena Williams said this was a match that held no fear factor for her, and in the opening set she was her own worst enemy. She compromised herself from the service line with seven double faults and blasted a forehand way wide of the sideline at set point. She had a lead throughout the tie breaker until Venus scooted in front, 5-4, thanks to a backhand blunder from the youngest but burliest Williams.

Both sisters were more proficient with their returns than with their serves in the first set, when they shared eight service breaks in 12 games. But in the second set, Serena, who wore green beads in her coif in honor of the Green Bay Packers and read some "Hamlet" to put herself in the mood for this intrafamily intrigue, was the sister who cracked first.

By the time Venus had sprinted ahead to a 3-0 lead, Serena had summoned a trainer to tape the sore right knee that hampered her campaign last week in Sydney, where she avoided a potential final-round clash with her sibling by bowing to the eventual champion, Arantxa Sanchez Vicario, in the semifinal round.

"Serena is a great player, and even though she hasn't played that much, she's been taking people out left and right," Venus said.

"Seeing her across the net was a little bit odd, but it's to be expected, and in the future it'll be the same."

Another Sister Showdown for Williamses

BY CHRISTOPHER CLAREY | MAY 8, 1998

ORACENE WILLIAMS WORE her usual uniform, a warm-up suit and sneakers, to the Italian Open today, which was altogether appropriate.

Keeping up with her daughters at the Foro Italico was no sedentary task. When the Round of 16 began in Rome today, Serena Williams was on center court to play the four-time Italian Open champion Conchita Martinez. Meanwhile, her senior sister and soul mate, Venus, was on the grandstand court to play Alexandra Fusai, the Frenchwoman who upset second-seeded Jana Novotna the previous afternoon.

While her daughters dashed across the red clay courts, Oracene dashed across the concourse attempting to stay aware of developments. "I think I covered more ground than they did," she said.

On Friday, Mom will be able to remain seated. Her daughters both won convincingly, which means they will play each other in the quarterfinals. It will be their second meeting as professionals. The first came in January in the second round of the Australian Open. Venus won, 7-6 (7-4), 6-1.

"For them to play so early in the tournament here is too bad," Oracene Williams said. "The good news is that one of them will still be in, but there really is no loser. They are one, so it doesn't matter."

Venus, 17, and Serena, 16, were practice partners long before they were teen-agers, and they were doubles partners today shortly after finishing their singles matches. Although Venus smacked her sister in the back with a big first serve late in the second set of their victory, it was purely coincidental. They are one.

"I guess I am kind of playing me a little bit, even though we're different," Venus said. "Anybody else doesn't play with me so often and live with me."

Serena took a more playful tack: "Actually I wanted to see Venus's match today to do some scouting, but I finished a little later than she did, so I'm not really sure how she plays," she said, having a harder time suppressing laughter than she did suppressing Martinez, 6-2, 6-2.

Both Serena and Venus, who beat Fusai, 6-1, 6-1, today, have improved since the Australian Open. "I had no type of backhand, but that is way in the past," said Serena Williams. "Actually, it's one of my strong points now. Hopefully, it will be a little different tomorrow."

This is the first Italian Open for the Williamses. They have had a glimpse of the Colosseum and are planning a visit to the Vatican and the Sistine Chapel. Serena even managed to answer one question in Italian at her news conference today. But on court, the sisters have been all business, with neither losing a set. Serena has had the much tougher draw here, beating 11th-seeded Nathalie Tauziat, 7-5, 6-0, in the first round.

Serena, now ranked 31st, has beaten six members of the top 10 in her short career. Today, she thoroughly dominated the seventh-seeded Martinez. The 26-year-old Spaniard thrives on clay and won this tournament four straight times before losing in last year's final, but she plays traditional clay court tennis, hitting heavy topspin with her forehand and stationing herself far behind the baseline. Serena is a thoroughly modern player who hits the ball early and ferociously. She dictated play from the outset and frequently stood five feet inside the baseline to hit winners off Martinez's soft second serve.

"I tell myself clay is my favorite surface," said Serena, now 3-0 on the stuff, "and when I get to Wimbledon, I'll say grass is my favorite surface."

Monica Seles is also thinking positively. Although she lost, 6-2, 4-6, 7-5, to France's Sandrine Testud, she has lost weight and gained enthusiasm in recent weeks. She has yet to regain her once-unwavering self-belief, however, and double-faulted seven times in the final set.

Continents Apart, Williams Sisters Make History

BY SAL A. ZANCA | MARCH 1, 1999

VENUS AND SERENA WILLIAMS became prodigies and then top-25 players together, traveling and playing as part of a family campaign that kept its distance from the tennis establishment. But the sisters had to travel almost 5,000 miles apart to make history.

Serena, 17 years old and ranked 24th in the world, took her first WTA Tour singles title today, winning the Gaz de France tournament here over Amelie Mauresmo of France, 6-2, 3-6, 7-6 (7-4). About five hours later, Venus, 18 years old and ranked No. 5, repeated as the winner of the IGA Superthrift Classic in Oklahoma City, beating Amanda Coetzer by 6-4, 6-0.

It was the first time that sisters had won tournaments in the same week on the WTA Tour. Two sisters played in finals on the same day in April 1991, but Manuela Maleeva lost in Spain and Magdalena Maleeva lost in Croatia.

Venus Williams's title was her fourth professional singles title. But Serena, who will move up to No. 21 in the ranking, could boast that she was three months younger than Venus was in winning her first singles title, taking it at 17 years 5 months. Serena needed 1 hour 57 minutes to defeat Mauresmo, another up-and-coming teen-ager, while Venus disposed of Coetzer in 58 minutes.

Serena said she tried unsuccessfully to talk to her sister before their matches today.

"I wasn't able to talk to her yet, but I did talk to my dad, who told me some things," said Serena, who won mixed doubles titles at Wimbledon and the United States Open last year. "I'll see Venus soon."

In Oklahoma City, Venus said, "I found out that she won before I came out to play the match, so I really felt that it was my duty to come out here and win."

During the week, the sisters traded E-mail messages to stay in touch. In the past they have not needed the Internet or long-distance telephone calls to communicate; they could just call across the locker room, and they have won three doubles titles playing together on the WTA Tour. But now they are trying different schedules, with their father, Richard, following one and their mother, Oracene, following the other.

In the Gaz de France final, Serena Williams and Mauresmo slugged it out, combining hits with nearly as many misses. At the end, it took a tie breaker to separate them in a match that may have shown the future of women's tennis.

It wasn't pretty — especially in the error-filled third set, when Williams wasted a 4-1 lead and could not serve out the match at 5-4, and Mauresmo double-faulted at important times — but the strength and all-round attacking games of both players showed that sticking strictly to the baseline may finally be a thing of the past.

Williams, who was playing in her first tour final, embraced her mother at the end of the match before accepting the trophy and making a short acceptance speech in French to the crowd of nearly 5,000, which from the start of the match was rooting for the 19-year-old Mauresmo.

Yet Williams was able to block it out. "It didn't bother me," she said. "I was just trying to think about what I had to do to win."

The sixth-seeded Mauresmo had become the French favorite after making it to the final of the Australian Open last month against Martina Hingis.

Hingis won that final, but lost to Mauresmo in the quarterfinals here on Friday in a bitter rematch. Both players tried to play down the controversy from the Australian Open, where Hingis called Mauresmo "half a man" after Mauresmo publicly acknowledged her homosexuality.

In today's match there was no bitterness, just hard — and harder — tennis. More than a few times, a winner drilled deep into the corner brought gasps from the crowd, but they were not for Mauresmo's feared backhand. Instead, it was Williams's two-handed backhand that drew an audible response.

After playing against her older and bigger sister nearly all her life, Williams was not awed by the 18th-ranked Mauresmo, who is 4 inches shorter and 27 pounds lighter than the 6-foot-1-inch, 169-pound Venus Williams.

"She really didn't hit that hard to me," Serena Williams, who was not seeded, said of Mauresmo. "Maybe because I am so used to power. She hit a nice ball, a deep ball with a lot of spin. But I really didn't feel too much power out there. Maybe because I was feeling so strong."

For more than a week, Mauresmo was built up by the French public and news media alike. She had not played since the Australian Open, and had vacationed in New Caledonia. She may have come back refreshed, but five matches in five days wore on her.

"I think she was a bit nervous, playing here at home," Williams said.

A number of times Williams sent Mauresmo stretching, and in the third set Mauresmo stopped trying for some returns.

Williams won the first set by taking the final four games, but Mauresmo won the second set and battled back from 1-4 in the third to force the tie breaker. Still, it was Williams who dominated at the end.

"I didn't like being down, 5-6," Williams said. "I really felt better when I was ahead. I just wanted to stay ahead and I decided if I want to win, if I wanted to be the best, I had better be able to close out the match."

She did, going ahead by 2-0 in the tie breaker with her 12th ace of the match. Although Mauresmo came back to even the tie breaker at 3-3, an approach and forehand volley gave Williams the lead for good. Leading by 5-3, Williams hit another ace to set up several match points.

The final point came on a Williams return that clipped the net and went over, throwing Mauresmo out of position. Mauresmo's shot went wide and Williams had the victory, which she celebrated by throwing her racquet after a moment of disbelief.

Richard Williams has said that he expects Serena to become a better player than her older and, so far, more accomplished sister; today, she narrowed the gap.

"This is a start for me," Serena said. "It's always good to get a smaller tournament under your belt so that by the time you get to the Slams, you have a lot of experience."

Playing in Draw's Opposite Sides Benefits the Williamses and the Game

BY ROBIN FINN | MARCH 21, 1999

THE MOST AMBITIOUS sister act ever to declare itself a sure bet for a total takeover of women's tennis has developed complications consistent with a head-on collision: fifth-ranked Venus Williams and 16th-ranked Serena Williams are gaining on an identical destination, the No. 1 ranking. Will one have to mow down the other to get there? Their parents suspect so.

"It's complicated enough just to have one champion around the house, but two, that's enough to break up a home," said Richard Williams, the father Frankenstein who masterminded this double assault, "but there's no stopping these girls."

Richard Williams began coaching his two youngest daughters on the pockmarked public courts of Compton, Calif., in their preschool years. Tennis was their ticket to a bigger, better life, and each sibling wanted in. This week at the Lipton Championships, in Key Biscayne, Fla., where Venus is the defending champion, both are seeded. To their father's delight, they landed in opposite halves of the draw.

"Everybody else out there better start moving over for the Williams girls, because they're pushing for No. 1 and No. 2 now," said Richard Williams, who predicts his daughters will monopolize the tour. "If tournament directors are smart, they're going to see the way these girls sell tickets and make sure they put them on different sides of the draw."

For him, a dream final and a nightmare final are one and the same: his two teen-agers duking it out for a title. They began their Lipton campaign yesterday, with 17-year-old Serena defeating Alicia Molik, a qualifier from Australia, 6-2, 6-3, and 18-year-old Venus beating the American Tara Snyder, 6-3, 6-4.

Having long outgrown the complications of Compton, where Williams made ends meet by running a security service, the family now calls a sprawling compound in Palm Beach Gardens, Fla., their happy home, not that they are home much anymore.

First, the family launched Venus, a United States Open finalist on her first try in 1997, and then came Serena, like her sister a collector of two Grand Slam mixed doubles titles and currently the owner of a tour-best unbeaten streak of 11 matches that yielded consecutive titles in Paris and Indian Wells, Calif. Thanks to their respective contracts with Reebok and Puma, neither sister has to worry where her next pair of sneakers is coming from.

Since one coach seemed insufficient for two rising stars, Richard Williams and his wife, Brandi, have divided the coaching duties between themselves the way garden variety families assign household chores: a fearful flyer, Richard has allowed his wife to handle most foreign events, including the Grand Slams, but he is always a phone call away. Just in case the all-in-the-family atmosphere threatens to become stifling, Nick Bollettieri volunteers his opinion, and motivational expertise. "Richard has his system working, he listens to advice, but he's done it all on his own," Bollettieri said. "The sky's the limit for those girls."

This season, aware that his daughters have demonstrated fearlessness in all competitive situations except the ones requiring them to tackle each other, Richard Williams is experimenting with a policy of avoidance at most non-Grand Slam events. It is his theory that his daughters will rack up titles quicker, and with less psychological distress, if they know they do not have to eliminate each other.

The strategy for minimizing sibling stress had a smash debut last month: Venus made a successful defense of her first career title in Oklahoma City, and Serena, to the surprise of everyone but her family, won her first title at Paris in her first career final.

The Williamses are the first pair of sisters to win separate titles on the same day and the first sisters since Bulgaria's Maleevas — Katerina, Manuela and Maggie — to rank simultaneously inside the top 20. Serena Williams broke into the top 20 last week in Indian Wells by winning the Evert Cup.

At Indian Wells, Venus acted as Serena's doubles and training partner but steered clear of the singles draw. Though both entered the Lipton, the sisters will be back in experimental mode in two weeks at the Bausch & Lomb Championships on Amelia Island, Fla., where Serena will take a back seat while Venus navigates the main draw. According to their father, they do not mind trading off, but he is not so sure he may not have an insurrection on his hands if he takes his theory to extremes.

"If it turns out that having them both playing singles in all the Slams hurts their results this year, I may start doing something different in the year 2000," he said. "I may allow both of them to play just two Slams. We'll see about how they feel about that one."

So far, the siblings have kept their rivalry to a simmer: Venus has beaten Serena in both meetings, then apologized. "I think Venus, when she puts her mind to it, is the most gifted female ever to play the game," Richard Williams boasted. "The only one who even comes close is Martina Navratilova."

Venus Williams has played along with his soundtrack, announcing there is nothing that is beyond her. "I believe I can do anything," she said, her eyes daring anyone to defy her, little sister included.

But lately, the little sister has not been listening. "I always believed I can beat the best, be the best, achieve the best," said Serena after downing Steffi Graf in the Indian Wells finale. "I always see myself in the top position."

May the best sister win.

U.S. Open; Unstoppable Team Williams Takes Doubles Title

BY ROBIN FINN | SEPT. 13, 1999

IT'S JUST LIKE Irving Berlin used to say: Sisters, sisters, there were never more devoted sisters. As soon as 17-year-old Serena Williams, who seized the United States Open singles championship and $750,000 Saturday night by throttling Martina Hingis, it was time to go back to the hardcourts and play more hardball. She and her best pal/big sister/doubles partner for life, 19-year-old Venus, had a doubles final to play.

"I don't want to let Venus down at all," said Serena, who didn't. She and Venus defeated unseeded Chanda Rubin and Sandrine Testud, 4-6, 6-1, 6-4, in the women's doubles final. After all, it was Venus, huddled in a hooded sweatshirt in the corner of the family box, who Serena looked to for emotional restoration upon letting a pair of championship points escape in her final against Hingis.

"I saw Venus over there really making sure, pumping me up; it really helped me," said Serena, relieved that her sibling, who she has never defeated in a professional match, didn't mind being beaten to the first Grand Slam singles crown on the family mantel.

But Serena said her sister's depression over not beating Hingis in the semis and create a Williams family dream final was a source of inspiration to hang tough against Hingis, the player who clamped down when Venus cramped up.

"I've never seen her that down before," said Serena, who described herself and her sister as "predominantly bitter" after each other's losses. "That really encouraged me to be even more tough out there, just to have to see her that down."

Yesterday, on a day that began with an early morning photo shoot in Central Park, Serena Williams ignored the 21 messages on her cell phone, put her game face on one more time and joined her sister for their doubles victory. They are the first sisters to win an Open doubles championship in 101 years, since Juliette and Kathleen Atkinson accomplished it in 1897 and 1898.

Besides partly fulfilling the prediction of their father, Richard, that this Open would see an all-Williams final, the sisters captured their second career Grand Slam doubles crown (the 1999 French Open was the first) and pocketed $330,000. In total, the Williams girls took $1.29 million to the bank for their two-week Open travail, $915,000 of it reeled in by the little sister.

"Whooo," yelped the big winner. "I guess Uncle Sam's really happy."

Talk about a packed agenda: besides winning her first Grand Slam title in her first Grand Slam final, Serena, now ranked fourth in the world, let it slip that, along with her crusade for Hingis's top spot, she would like to flex her muscles in a different arena and rival Minnesota Gov. Jesse Ventura's legacy in the wrestling ring. Surrounded by puppies, the latest of them a Jack Russell terrier named Jackie that accompanied her on the court for the doubles award ceremony, Williams has also expressed a desire to become a veterinarian someday.

Just before the fifth-seeded Williams sisters reached yesterday's final with a straight-set dismissal of 12th-seeded Mary Pierce and Barbara Schett late Saturday night, Serena swapped college talk with Chelsea Clinton, on the party line with her father, President Clinton, for a congratulations call.

The outcome of that was an invitation to the White House and the offer of a guided tour of Stanford from Chelsea when Serena hits town this week for the Fed Cup championship against Russia.

Still giddy from her singles and doubles sweep, Serena said she was considering entering the men's event next year, just for the challenge of it. When she realized she still hadn't had time to celebrate her championship, her slightly subdued sibling piped in.

"She'll celebrate with her credit card," Venus said.

Williams Sisters Learned to Think Off Court, Too

BY SELENA ROBERTS | JULY 3, 2000

IT WAS EARLY in the fortnight, and Richard Williams was crisscrossing the grounds with a cigarette dangling from his lips, shaking random thoughts from his head like Tic-Tacs. Did he mention his screenplay, his plans for a magazine, his interests in cashing in on the Internet?

"I'm into Webcasting," Williams said. "If Serena and Venus went into that business, they'd make more money in two years than they would in 50 of doing something else. If it was up to me, I'd like to see them retire right now and move on. Let's go."

It's just a suggestion, though. At the same time that Tour parents like Damir Dokic and Samantha Stevenson appeared on the grounds of the All England Club like Svengalis for their children — either feeding them answers to questions or hovering over their every move during the first week of Wimbledon — it became more apparent that Richard and Oracene Williams have raised two independent thinkers.

They still call Richard Williams Daddy, but as Serena and Venus Williams exit their teens one by one, both have been encouraged to inch into adulthood. With built-in filters for parental advice, they have begun to make their own decisions.

"It depends on what decision it is," said Venus Williams, who turned 20 two weeks ago. "My parents have taught us to make decisions on our own, to be independent. But on certain things, we still go, 'Can we do this?' It's quite odd."

But normal, too. Sometimes, normal seems in short supply on the Tour. So does perspective, and this is a trait Venus and Serena Williams use deftly when it comes to their father's techno-career dreams for them.

"When you're real good at something, it's tough to say goodbye, especially if it's something you've done all your life," said Venus

Williams, who, like Serena, will begin Week 2 of Wimbledon with a Round of 16 match today. "I suppose I'll be around a little while more. No more retirement scares at this point.

"I'd get bored in an office, just sitting around, eating doughnuts."

She knows herself well. Early last week her father told a story about how Venus used to stare out the window of her second-grade classroom, with the sound of the lecture as background noise for her daydreams.

"The teacher said to me, 'Your daughter has no interest in school; she's always looking out the window,' " Richard Williams said. "I thought she was kidding, but I got up on top of the building and saw her looking out the window. I asked Venus why, and she said, 'Everything they're doing, I did in first grade.' "

On a tour where education is sometimes squeezed in between photo ops, practice time, travel schedules and matches, the articulate Williams sisters do seem advanced. They enjoy the learning process — even on the court. They have heard past criticisms about their games — too much power, not enough strategy — and have been open to change.

"We have a different game than when we first came out," said Serena Williams, who will be 19 in September. "We have a lot of power, whereas someone who doesn't have it has to do different things. But I think now I have added strategy to my game."

They have not altered their flair, though. They are still as free spirited and shoulder high in self-esteem as when they arrived on the scene, but they were a calm core amid the lunacy that whirled around them last week. On the same day Jelena Dokic's ranting father was led away by the police, an accusation of a racial slur was leveled by Alexandra Stevenson, and Alexandra's mother, Samantha, described a physical confrontation with a French player, the Williams sisters would not be baited into the fray.

In the past, Serena Williams has denied any encounters of overt racism on the Tour, but she was politically aware enough to take a stand against the Confederate flag in South Carolina, refusing to play in the state. On Friday night, a day after Alexandra Stevenson's claim, Serena Williams was asked again if she had been confronted with racism.

"I've already covered that question," she said. "You can get the transcripts."

The sisters are quick witted, sometimes coy, but often viewed as aloof. Yet their standoffishness seems born out of a survival instinct. Last week, Stevenson described hazing she said she received from fellow players she believed were jealous of her celebrity. While the Williams sisters have been celebrated on magazine covers and in television features, they do not take notes on who loves or loathes them. Steering clear of gossip, they keep their distance from other players.

"I'm always around my mom, my dad and Venus," Serena Williams said. "Just stick close to yourself and be not too friendly. That's why a lot of people have a problem with us, because we're not too friendly with anyone. We're cordial, say, 'Hi,' and et cetera."

They are not motivated by popularity, steered by cliques or unnerved by sister envy. When Week 2 of Wimbledon begins, Venus and Serena Williams will be on track to accomplish the same thing: win at Wimbledon. Last summer, Serena won the United States Open title while Venus sat emotionally detached from the moment. At that point, the issue of sibling rivalry took root. On Saturday, Venus Williams handled the issue the same way she does most others, with maturity.

"I don't even think we have sibling rivalry in our heart," she said. "Whatever we share, we share the best we can. I don't think it's inside of us. Does it really matter who won a Grand Slam first? She played better. It's my loss. It's her win. It's all in the Williams family."

It is a family that is tight, and yet Richard and Oracene Williams have given their daughters room to grow. Their daughters recently moved into their own home. And during a week when parents trampled the bounds of control, the sisters stood out as glowing examples of independence. "My dad always talks about his mom," said Serena

Williams, whose grandmother was a sharecropper. "He always talks about how she helped him be the person that he is. He's a very positive person. He's really outgoing and really he's like—I wish I could describe him. He's very determined. I just imagine my grandmother to be the same way.

"I never really got a chance to know her very well, but from all the stuff that he says and the things that he does, usually the apple doesn't fall far from the tree."

The Williamses, Reluctant Rivals, Will Battle for the French Title

BY SELENA ROBERTS | JUNE 8, 2002

VENUS AND SERENA WILLIAMS worked their way down the lunch line linked as closely as paper dolls, side by side as they inspected the cafeteria spread, inseparable as they searched out a table.

Moments earlier, they had been hitting together on a practice court at Roland Garros. Now they were laughing together over lunch. Sisterhood as usual. But on Saturday, they will step into the finals of the French Open and try on the skin of strangers.

If this meeting is anything like the others, they won't make eye contact on the changeovers, acknowledge a good shot of the other or let a bad line call go without an argument.

But try as they might, they have never competed without genetic baggage. Blood dilutes their killer instincts. Kinship takes the edge off the overheads.

"They haven't played up to their potential," their mother, Oracene Williams, said of their face-to-face encounters. "There might be a barrier. They are sisters. You can't neglect that fact."

Spy novels are laced with fewer plots than the debate surrounding an all-Williams final. If one doesn't play well, it must be the other's turn to win. If one unleashes more unforced errors, it must be part of a family strategy. Many players believe it, some onlookers swear by it and Jennifer Capriati only added to it with her collusion theories after losing to Serena in the semifinals. According to her logic, even the sisters' ascent to No. 1 and No. 2 in the ranking is probably by design.

"Wishful thinking," Oracene Williams said with a smile.

In reality, the sisters' unbelievable rise in the ranking, but uninspiring play against each other, is less a sinister plan and more the product of the subconscious. To have no mercy against other opponents is one thing, but to prey on a sister's vulnerable moment is another.

They have played seven matches against each other, with Venus winning five of them. None have left anyone spellbound by the level of play.

That could change this time. There is a chance that after enough time as opponents on grand stages, Venus and Serena will find a rhythm that will manufacture at least a few compelling points.

There is a chance the one in a groove will be Serena. In the three years since she won the United States Open, becoming the first of the two sisters to nab a major, she has watched Venus capture four major titles. The 2001 United States Open was Venus's last, a title she accepted on the court with her arm draped around Serena, the crestfallen runner-up.

"This time, I'd like to see Serena get one since she hasn't had one since 1999," Oracene Williams said.

Serena may be in position to do it. On the clay surface, she has compact steps, bursts of speed and the ability to slide. On a drop-volley shot that she got against Capriati on Thursday, Serena left the skid mark of a getaway car.

Angular in body style, Venus isn't built for clay. She has the wingspan of a condor and the speed to match, but her loping strides and reluctance to slide may leave her with a disadvantage.

The tale of the tape aside, Serena may simply be hungrier than Venus for the French Open title and more serious about tennis than she has been in the past few years.

"Right now, I really want to win the French Open, and I'm sure she does, too," Serena said. "I think in the beginning, maybe for me, it was a bit tougher to play her because of me being the younger sister. But now, I'm just ... I'm really ... I want to win a Grand Slam more than anything.

"I think at the U.S. Open, I was too caught up with getting back to the finals."

Serena's emotions tend to surface quicker than Venus's. Her nerves are more transparent, too. This spring, Serena has proven less vulnerable to the turns of her stomach that have overwhelmed her in the past.

Not only did she brush Venus aside in Key Biscayne, Fla., with a straight-set victory early this spring, she came back against Capriati in two tense matches. On Thursday, she made it a third, outlasting Capriati once again.

"Serena has been playing really well, intensity level, running well," Venus said. "We've practiced a lot on clay. I guess we'll be running down a lot of balls."

That is the hope. Long points, passionate rallies, an exciting final. Usually, that's not too much to expect of the No. 1 and No. 2 players in the world. But sisters make complicated adversaries, a fact underscored by Venus's wish for Serena to find as much success as she has.

"Actually, I'd like to stay No. 1, but I'd like to see Serena No. 1 also," Venus said. "I'm not giving it up, but I'm sure she'll get there."

Either way, they'll be side by side, with no sign of jealousy in between.

"It's just a sport," Oracene said. "What it is, tennis is on the court. Off the court, we don't even talk about it."

Williamses' Rivalry Is Close and Compelling, if Not Classic

BY CHRISTOPHER CLAREY | JULY 5, 2008

WIMBLEDON, ENGLAND — On Friday, Venus and Serena Williams were side by side on the English grass, applauding each other's winners and then pirouetting in unison as they waved to the crowd after advancing to the final of the women's doubles at Wimbledon.

On Saturday, they will be facing each other across the net for the singles trophy.

Such abrupt changes of mood and role have been a part of the Williamses' existence since they were children learning the game in Compton, Calif. They would shift from playmates off the court to combatants on it for the duration of their practice matches.

"Venus was nothing but legs; Serena was nothing but muscle, and I would encourage Serena because she would lose all the time," Oracene Price, their mother and co-coach, said in an interview at the All England Club. "And I'd say: 'Serena, just believe it. You can do it. Stop doubting yourself.' Because she looked up to Venus so much. And finally, she started doing it, but it wasn't until they started playing professional that she really started doing it."

On paper, their sibling sports rivalry has grown into a close and compelling one. Since it began with a Venus victory and a shared bow to the crowd in the second round of the Australian Open in 1998, they have played a total of 15 times as professionals. Serena has won eight, including six in a row during a particularly lopsided phase in 2002 and 2003.

But for those who have actually sat through their many close encounters, the effect has often been underwhelming. The unforced errors have piled up and the fans have felt conflicted. The psychological forces at work have often made it difficult for the sisters to fully express their games and their personalities. Meanwhile, their tactically similar games have made it difficult to generate the stylistic contrasts that have been the appeal of rivalries like the one between Martina Navratilova and Chris Evert, considered the gold standard in women's tennis.

The sisters are aware of these perceptions, and Serena was quick to rebut the suggestion that she and Venus have yet to play a classic final, pointing to the 2002 United States Open final, played under the lights in New York, and the 2003 Australian Open final, played indoors because of extreme heat. Serena won those encounters. "I think you're stating opinions," she said. "I've had a very classic Grand Slam final against her at the Australian Open. It was three extremely tough sets. It was a long match. It wasn't very easy. And I think also at the U.S. Open, it was fast, but it was very high-quality tennis. So I look forward to it."

Their last Grand Slam meeting, in the fourth round of the United States Open in 2005, was not on Serena's short list. She was out of shape and sorts and was beaten in two awkward sets, 7-6 (5), 6-2.

Their last joint Grand Slam final, won by Serena at Wimbledon in 2003 in three sets, was also anticlimactic, because Venus played with a strained abdominal muscle that forced her to leave the court for additional treatment and that visibly hampered her in the final set. Venus said then that one of the main reasons she played was that she did not want to generate any more debate about whether she and Serena arranged their matches in advance. The sisters have always dismissed such claims.

"It hasn't been easy," Venus said after the 2003 final. "Serena and I have been blamed for a lot of things that never even happened. I felt today I had to play."

The issue resurfaced briefly after Thursday's women's semifinals, when Venus's opponent, Elena Dementieva, said that the upcoming all-Williams final would be "a family decision." Dementieva later issued a statement denying that she had intended to imply that the result would be fixed, but the subject still received substantial coverage.

"They have never fixed a match," Price said. "Why would they do something like that? They are both competitive people. Serena is as serious as a heart attack. But I'm not surprised that this still comes up. People are always looking for something negative."

The question now is whether this latest final, their seventh in a Grand Slam, will turn into something more positive. Venus, the defending champion, leads in Wimbledon titles with four to Serena's two, but Serena has eight overall Grand Slam singles titles to Venus's six. Serena has also won all four of the majors, while Venus's titles have all come at Wimbledon and the United States Open.

Richard Williams, their father and co-coach, says this match will be close, but he will not be in London to see it. He flew to Florida on Friday because he gets overwrought watching his daughters face off.

"He said he did his job, and his job was done," Serena said. "No matter what happens, he's for sure going to be a winner."

Price, now divorced from Richard Williams, will be at Centre Court. She said she was convinced that it had not gotten easier for her daughters to play each other.

"No, because Serena is more competitive than ever," Price said with a laugh. "Venus, when it comes to her sister, is more relaxed. But Serena, if she could win every one, she would and not feel anything."

Price said she believed that her daughters' limited tennis schedules and outside interests had helped them have longer careers than some of their now-retired former rivals, like Justine Henin and Martina Hingis.

"I know some of those players were just living and breathing tennis," Price said. "You can't keep going like that for too long. If that's all you do, you're going to burn out."

Although the sisters still share a house in Palm Beach Gardens, Fla., and are sharing a house at Wimbledon, they often practice separately, working with their own male hitting partners. Serena works with the German Sasha Bajin, Venus with the former American tour player David Witt.

"I think that what makes it difficult when they hit together is that they both want to work on their own stuff, just like any other player would," Witt said.

The mood was certainly not light and jovial as the sisters gave a joint news conference on Friday, with neither Venus nor Serena in a particularly communicative mood after defeating Nathalie Dechy of France and Casey Dellacqua of Australia, 6-3, 6-3. Asked if it had gotten any easier to play singles against each other, Serena answered: "The opponent hasn't gotten any easier, that's for sure. So it's going to be a battle again. That's just how it is."

A Final Match for Venus and Serena Williams. But Maybe Not the Last One.

BY CHRISTOPHER CLAREY | JAN. 26, 2017

MELBOURNE, AUSTRALIA — The sibling rivalry, at least on the tennis tour, started right here at the Australian Open for the Williams sisters.

It was 1998, and older sister Venus beat younger sister Serena, 7-6 (4), 6-1, in a second-round match that — as intrusive as it felt to watch — surely drew more attention than any second-round match in history between a pair of Australian Open debutantes.

The fascination in their dynamic and their futures was there from the start in Melbourne Park, known then as Flinders Park when it had only one stadium with a retractable roof instead of three. A picture of Venus consoling Serena after the match was on the front page of The New York Times.

Though it would be tempting to label their Australian Open final on Saturday as a full-circle moment and to speculate that it might be their last meeting at this late a stage of a Grand Slam tournament, it seems best to resist the temptation.

The Williams sisters have taught us a lot about the limits of conventional tennis wisdom through the years. And so, even if 19 years have passed and Serena is now 35 and Venus 36, it is wise to avoid fencing them in again after they have run roughshod over so many other preconceptions.

"I watched Venus today celebrating after she won the semifinal like she was a 6-year-old girl, and it made you want to cry for joy just watching her," said Marion Bartoli, a former Wimbledon champion. "Such a powerful image, and it makes you think about all those questions she was getting: 'When are you retiring? Have you thought about retiring? How much longer?'

"You must let the champions decide when the right moment comes."

The Williamses are both great champions, even if Serena is clearly the greater player with her 22 Grand Slam singles titles and her long run at No. 1, a spot she can reclaim from Angelique Kerber with a win Saturday.

Serena has been the most prolific Grand Slam winner after age 30 in tennis history, and she is back in rare form again after another extended break at the end of 2016. She disconnected completely from the game and physical training initially and had to push hard to get back in shape in November and December.

It worked. She has not dropped a set here despite a challenging draw, nor has she even been pushed to a tiebreaker. Newly engaged to the American technology entrepreneur Alexis Ohanian, who has watched her matches from the players box, and seemingly refreshed, Serena deserves to be the favorite to win her 23rd major singles title and break her tie with Steffi Graf for the highest total in the Open era.

In this tournament, Serena has beaten two former members of the top 10 — Belinda Bencic and Lucie Safarova — and one current member, the in-form No. 9 seed Johanna Konta. Venus's draw has been soft by comparison, devoid of top 10 players — past or present — and including only one seeded player: No. 24 Anastasia Pavlyuchenkova.

On Thursday, she had to scrap and come back to win, 6-7 (3), 6-2, 6-3, against the powerful unseeded American CoCo Vandeweghe, while Serena cruised past the unseeded Croat Mirjana Lucic-Baroni, 6-2, 6-1.

Serena, who already holds a 16-11 edge over her sister, could be the fresher player, too, on Saturday. But the psychology remains complex and the fallout unpredictable, even after all these years.

"When I'm playing on the court with her, I think I'm playing the best competitor in the game," Venus said. "I don't think I'm chump change either, you know. I can compete against any odds. No matter what, I can get out there, and I compete."

They have not played since the 2015 United States Open, when Serena won, 6-2, 1-6, 6-3, in a quarterfinal in which Venus attacked, often successfully, from the start but had no answer in the end for Serena's ultimate weapon: her first serve.

It was an intense match in which the big crowd in Arthur Ashe Stadium seemed more reflective than fully engaged; one in which Serena's celebration was understandably subdued with her sister across the net, even if their matches are no longer the awkward, constricted affairs of their early years.

Saturday's final in Melbourne could be intriguing on multiple levels, in part because of the Australian public. Venus is viewed here, as elsewhere, as a sympathetic figure: the older sister who has handled the younger's greater tennis success unselfishly and with dignity. And though both sisters have had to cope with major health problems and family tragedy, with the murder of their half sister Yetunde Price in 2003, Venus is the one whose tennis fortunes dipped more dramatically.

A seven-time Grand Slam singles champion and a former No. 1, she did not advance past the third round in any major event in singles from late 2011 to the end of the 2014 season.

She was a major star reduced to a minor role, largely because of an autoimmune disorder — Sjogren's syndrome, diagnosed in 2011 — that sapped her strength and endurance. When Russian hackers breached the World Anti-Doping Agency's databases last fall, it was revealed that Venus had needed 13 therapeutic-use exemptions for drugs in recent years.

The retirement questions to which Bartoli referred started during that period. But Venus's ability to cope with her condition has improved, and after rejoining the top 10 in 2015, she reached the semifinals at Wimbledon last year and then the final here.

"She never even thought of the word retire," said David Witt, her coach and hitting partner of 10 years. "I just think when she got diagnosed, it was a step back, a shock. She's learned a lot about how to deal with it and her body, how to eat, how to manage it.

SAM HODGSON FOR THE NEW YORK TIMES

Venus Williams embraces her sister Serena after losing to her in the quarterfinals of the women's singles at the United States Open at Arthur Ashe Stadium.

"There are days she can't work as hard as she wants to work. Some days it's maybe not smart to do it because it will then hurt you for two or three more days. Where she is now in her career, she has to listen to her body, and I don't think she really needs to go out and hit balls for two hours."

Witt said there were no more two-a-day sessions in the off-season or in time off tour: just one session in the morning and then gym work, primarily sprints, core strengthening and flexibility.

"It took her years and years to realize that stretching is important and can keep you healthier," he said. "The more flexible you are, you're not going to strain or pull anything. I've been with her 10 years, and I think it took seven years to get her to stretch. She likes to do a lot of dancing, and that consists of a lot of stretching and being flexible, so I think that's helped."

Her dance skills were in evidence Thursday as she pirouetted after beating Vandeweghe, but what will linger longest in memory were her screams of delight at having conquered an inspired young opponent in a semifinal. It was a moment she described as "just joy."

"You could really see the happiness on her face," Serena said. "I've been there when she was down and out of it, and back and in it. I've been there for all those moments, so I just really was oh so happy."

As visceral as her reaction on court was, she was nothing but considered in the interview room.

"I think why people love sport so much is because you see everything in a line," Venus said. "In that moment, there is no do-over. There's no retake. There is no voice-over. It's triumph and disaster witnessed in real time.

"This is why people live and die for sport, because you can't fake it. You can't. It's either you do it or you don't. People relate to the champion. They also relate to the person who didn't win, because we all have those moments in our life."

This will be Venus's first major singles final since she lost to Serena in straight sets in the 2009 Wimbledon final, and her first match against Serena in Melbourne since the 2003 final when Serena won her fourth Grand Slam title in a row, having defeated Venus in all four finals.

"It's just amazing," said Rennae Stubbs, the Australian star who first met the sisters before they joined the tour. "They came onto the scene at age 15 and 16 with the beads and the hair and the exuberance, and here they are: mature, remarkable young women at 35 and 36. No matter what anyone says to me, their story from start to finish is the greatest sports story ever."

And if the Williamses have taught us anything along the way, it is that the story is not finished until they say it is.

Grand Sibling Rivalry Leaves Venus Williams a Distinct Underdog

BY VICTOR MATHER AND NAILA-JEAN MEYERS | JAN. 27. 2017

IS IT 2002 AGAIN?

The final of the Australian Open on Saturday was set to feature the American sisters Venus and Serena Williams together at the end — a common sight a decade or more ago. The sisters had played in eight Grand Slam finals entering Saturday, but not since 2009.

Not every fan has pined for the return of the Williams rivalry. Their matches are often criticized as passionless, and the sisters have said they do not especially enjoy playing each other.

"It definitely doesn't get easier," Serena said after an early-round match between them at Wimbledon in 2015.

Here are their previous eight Grand Slam finals, six of which were won by Serena.

2001 U.S. OPEN: VENUS IN TWO SETS

Venus Williams, 21, was already a three-time major winner and the defending champion. Serena, 19, had precociously won the Open two years before but had not been back to a Grand Slam final since. In the Open's first prime-time women's final, the older sister won, 6-2, 6-4. It was the first major Grand Slam final between sisters since Maud and Lilian Watson at Wimbledon in 1884 and also the first to feature two African-Americans.

How long ago was it? In the men's final, Lleyton Hewitt defeated Pete Sampras.

THE WINNER SAID: "I always want Serena to win. It's strange. I'm the bigger sister. I'm the one who takes care of her. I make sure she has everything even if I don't. I love her. It's hard."

THE TIMES SAID: "There was no doubt about the effort as they grunted and grimaced through every point."

2002 FRENCH OPEN: SERENA IN TWO SETS

Serena experienced the longest major title drought of her career between her first in 1999 and her second here. After winning her first French Open, 7-5, 6-3, Serena would not win another at Roland Garros for 11 years. Venus has not advanced past the quarterfinals in Paris since.

THE WINNER SAID: "I was really fighting for this for so long. At one point, I wouldn't get past the quarters; then I got to the final, maybe a semi here and there. But it was just kind of discouraging. I didn't want to be a one-hit wonder."

THE TIMES SAID: "Today, the Williams sisters reversed roles. Serena held on, while Venus came undone."

CHANG W. LEE/THE NEW YORK TIMES

Venus Williams, center, after defeating her younger sister, Serena, left, in the 2001 United States Open final. "I love her. It's hard," Williams said after her victory.

2002 WIMBLEDON: SERENA IN TWO SETS

Serena followed her first French Open title with her first Wimbledon title, 7-6 (4), 6-3. Venus had been the two-time defending champion, and after this match, she lost the No. 1 ranking to Serena, too.

THE WINNER SAID: "I kept thinking to myself: 'O.K., Serena, just stay calm. Venus already has two Wimbledons. Try to fight.' "

THE TIMES SAID: "Playing with the ferocity normally reserved only for others, Venus and Serena discarded their sibling code of conduct during today's Wimbledon final."

2002 U.S. OPEN: SERENA IN TWO SETS

With a 6-4, 6-3 victory in Flushing Meadows, Serena completed a 4-0 season against her sister. Winning her third major in a row, Serena also tied Venus with four Grand Slam titles over all.

"Everybody has a year," Venus said. "This is her year. Next year could be her year, too."

THE WINNER SAID: "I prefer to play Venus because that means that we have reached our maximum potential and that we'll both go home winners. For me, I'm happy to play her in the final."

THE TIMES SAID: "If Venus and Serena continue to find each other at the end of majors the way Pete Sampras and Andre Agassi have all these years, there will be a universal appreciation for a rivalry that will never be re-created again."

2003 AUSTRALIAN OPEN: SERENA IN THREE SETS

For the fourth straight Grand Slam event, it was Williams versus Williams. And for the fourth straight time, Serena was the winner, completing her first so-called Serena Slam. For the first time, the match went three sets: 7-6 (4), 3-6, 6-4. (Serena completed another Serena Slam in 2014-15 by winning four majors in a row.)

THE WINNER SAID: "I never get choked up, never, but I'm really emotional right now and really, really happy."

THE TIMES SAID: "In a breathtaking, fist-pumping, title-gobbling hurry, Serena Williams has become one of the greats."

2003 WIMBLEDON: SERENA IN THREE SETS

After an all-Belgian French Open final between Kim Clijsters and Justine Henin, normal service resumed in the next major tournament. But this may have been the most awkward of the finals between the Williams sisters. Venus strained an abdominal muscle during her semifinal match, and later acknowledged that she might not have played if it had not been a Wimbledon final and if the opponent had not been her sister. Still, Venus battled for three sets, losing, 4-6, 6-4, 6-2.

THE WINNER SAID: "I was just telling myself, if anything, 'This is Wimbledon.' God knows if I would get this opportunity again, so I just kept telling myself that. I think, if anything, I fought harder."

THE TIMES SAID: "It might be getting easier for Serena to play her older sister, but it is still not nearly the same as matching huge ground strokes and healthy egos with an outsider. Playing Venus when she was injured only added a layer of complexity."

2008 WIMBLEDON: VENUS IN TWO SETS

After the sisters played each other six times in eight major finals from 2001 to 2003, it took almost five years for them to meet in a final again. For the first time since their first Grand Slam final, Venus came out on top, 7-5, 6-4. It was Venus's fifth Wimbledon title and seventh major championship over all, though she has not won one since.

THE WINNER SAID: "She played so awesome. It was really a task to beat her."

THE TIMES SAID: "Sisters for life and doubles partners later in the afternoon, Venus and Serena Williams put most of that aside for nearly two hours on Saturday at Wimbledon, smacking serves and ground strokes in each other's direction with a vengeance and an accuracy that have often been lacking in their previous family reunions."

2009 WIMBLEDON: SERENA IN TWO SETS

Venus was the two-time defending champion, and coming into the final, she had won 20 straight matches and 34 straight sets at the All England Club. But Serena would not be denied, winning, 7-6 (3), 6-2. She had claimed three of the past four Grand Slam events to bring her career total to 11.

THE WINNER SAID: (Of the Venus Rosewater Dish, presented to the winner) "It's named the Venus, and she always wins it, and it's just like wow. It hasn't settled in that I won yet."

THE TIMES SAID: "Serena's victory on Saturday, in which she finished with 12 aces and never lost her serve, was the latest confirmation that she is on another memorable run."

Serena Williams was not nearly done. Since that final, she has made 14 more, winning 11 for a career total of 22 Grand Slam singles championships. Venus has not been back to a final, with just two Grand Slam semifinal appearances.

Until this week. Seeded just 13th, Venus rolled back the years to seize an unexpected berth in the final in Melbourne. Once again, her sister stands in the way.

In Serena Williams's Comeback, a Familiar Opponent: Venus

BY CHRISTOPHER CLAREY | MARCH 10, 2018

INDIAN WELLS, CALIF. — In the first singles tournament of her comeback, Serena Williams will pick up where she left off by facing her older sister Venus in the third round of the BNP Paribas Open.

In Serena's last tournament before maternity leave, she defeated Venus in the final of the 2017 Australian Open. Venus was one of the few who were aware that her sister was two months pregnant.

Serena then spent 14 months away from the game.

Venus went on to have one of the finest seasons of her career in the major events in 2017, returning to the top 10 and providing further proof that being deep into your 30s is no barrier to excellence in professional tennis.

Serena said she could not watch.

"I get too nervous," she said. "If she makes a mistake, a little bit of me dies, so yeah, I didn't watch any."

But the sisters are back on tour together again, and both advanced by winning second-round matches on Saturday.

Venus Williams, seeded eighth, went first, defeating Sorana Cirstea, 6-3, 6-4, to record her first tour victory of 2018. Serena Williams went next, beating No. 29 seed Kiki Bertens, 7-6 (5), 7-5, in a tight match full of high-velocity rallies and abrupt shifts in momentum.

"I'm just so happy to be out here," Serena Williams said. "Everything is a bonus."

Now, she and her sister will face each other for the first time at the Indian Wells Tennis Garden, 17 years after a match that they were scheduled to play here failed to materialize.

"I literally didn't even think about it," Serena Williams said on Saturday. "That's, you know, totally gone out of my mind. First of all, 17 years ago seems like forever ago. Yikes."

It was supposed to be a semifinal in 2001, but Venus withdrew only a few minutes before the match was to begin, citing tendinitis in her right knee.

The late decision sparked conjecture that her withdrawal had been a family arrangement, a conspiracy theory given further momentum when the Russian player Elena Dementieva said after her quarterfinal loss to Venus Williams that she believed the sisters' father and coach, Richard Williams, decided who would win their matches.

The sisters and Richard Williams have denied that any such arrangement took place in Indian Wells, and Dementieva later insisted she had been joking.

But when Richard Williams and Venus Williams arrived at the stadium two days later to watch Serena Williams play the 2001 final against Kim Clijsters, they were met with a chorus of boos from the crowd of nearly 16,000 as the father and his daughter walked down the stairs to their courtside seats.

Richard Williams said he heard racial slurs directed at him, telling USA Today: "One said, 'I wish it was '75, we'd skin you alive.' I think Indian Wells disgraced America."

No other spectator present that day has confirmed publicly that such statements were made. But after Serena Williams defeated Clijsters to win her second singles title at Indian Wells, she did not return to the tournament until 2015. Venus did not end her boycott until the following year.

But this year, with Serena now 36 and Venus now 37, they are finally set to play in the California desert.

The third-round match will be their earliest meeting in a tour event since their first duel as professionals, when Venus Williams won, 7-6 (4), 6-1, in the second round of the 1998 Australian Open.

"I think it's a huge difference to play her in the semifinals or even the quarterfinals or a final as opposed to a third round," Serena Williams said. "We can always stay in the tournament longer if the both of us are in the tournament. And having to play each other in the third round, one of us is going to be gone. So it's definitely a lot easier to play later on."

They have faced each other repeatedly at the other most significant American tournaments, five times at the United States Open, four times in Key Biscayne, Fla., at the tournament now known as the Miami Open.

They have played in nine Grand Slam singles finals, with Serena winning seven of them. But Indian Wells has had to wait, and this duel comes at a unique moment in the sisters' careers with Serena, a 23-time Grand Slam singles champion, unseeded and unranked after her long layoff but clearly still a threat after defeating Zarina Diyas and Bertens in the first two rounds without losing a set.

"She's playing really well and just honing her game," said Venus Williams, who watched the Diyas match from the stands. "When she's missing, it's not by much."

That was not always the case on Saturday against Bertens as Serena Williams missed some serves by considerable margins and mistimed a few groundstrokes that landed far off the mark. Bertens is a dangerous if erratic opponent, quite capable of handling Williams's power and providing plenty of her own.

Her average first- and second-serve speeds were superior to Williams's on Saturday, and she tried and failed to serve for the opening set before Williams eventually prevailed in a tiebreaker.

Williams served unsuccessfully for the match at 5-4 in the second set, then rebounded to win the final two games, rallying from 15-40 on her serve to close out the victory by winning a series of extended rallies.

She is not yet in prime form, not yet in prime shape, but in her first two matches she has proved she still has staying power, coming to the net effectively, something she appears to be emphasizing in this comeback, and playing the crucial points with trademark intensity.

But all-Williams matches have never been exclusively about the tennis or the tactics. They are emotionally and psychologically fraught. The sisters remain extremely close and played doubles together just last month during a Fed Cup match against the Netherlands in Asheville, N.C.

"Obviously I wish it was anybody else in the draw, literally anybody, but that's O.K.," Serena Williams said of their latest rematch. "Just have to go out there and see how I am and do my best."

On the Doubles Court, Venus and Serena Williams Make Time Stand Still

BY CHRISTOPHER CLAREY | JUNE 1, 2018

PARIS — Virginie Razzano once spoiled Serena Williams's French Open, producing one of the biggest upsets in the Open era by defeating Williams in the first round in 2012.

But Williams had tennis's version of the last word on this drizzly Friday at Roland Garros. While Razzano was announcing her retirement at age 35 on the same Chatrier Court where she once generated those shock waves, Williams and her big sister Venus were chatting on their way back to the locker room after winning their second-round doubles match over Sara Errani and Kirsten Flipkens, 6-4, 6-2, on Court 7.

As the years pile up, the Williams sisters' peer group on tour continues to shrink. They won the first of their 14 Grand Slam doubles titles together here in 1999. Venus was 18 and Serena 17, and they defeated two other teenagers with sky-high profiles, Anna Kournikova and Martina Hingis, 6-3, 6-7 (2), 8-6, in the final.

Kournikova, now 36, has not played on tour since 2003; Hingis, 37, retired for the third and presumably final time last year as a doubles specialist. All of the sisters' other opponents in that 1999 doubles tournament are also retired — some long gone, like Lindsay Davenport and Mary Pierce.

Of the 128 women in the 1999 French Open singles tournament, only the Williamses played singles in Paris this year.

Despite many predictions that Venus's and Serena's careers would be brilliant but relatively short — one of those doing the predicting was Richard Williams, their father and coach — the sisters remain the best sibling act in sports, nearly 20 years later.

"It's really tough when you play one Williams," Venus once said. "When you play two, it's really not an easy win."

It is easy to imagine them eventually dropping the mic together.

"I know, we could do a double whammy," Serena told me recently. "It would be weird because we would both have to win or do something special at the same time. Maybe we'll do doubles."

That would be a fitting finish: one last run to a Wimbledon or a United States Open title together — with both in their early 40s, maybe — and the whole extended and sometimes divided Williams clan reunited in the players box.

"Venus loves being out on the tour, and I do, too," Serena said. "But also, I am loving being with Olympia, so I don't know."

Serena was referring to her infant daughter, born last September. For now, what she and Venus both know is that tennis is still worth the trouble: worth the soreness and even the post-match news conferences, although Serena is generally a lot more expansive than her sister these days.

They could well go deep in the doubles this year even if their coaches would probably prefer that they focus their energies on singles at this stage of their careers.

Only Serena has to worry about saving enough energy for singles at this stage of the French Open. While Venus lost in the first round, Serena has advanced to the third in her first Grand Slam tournament in 16 months and faces another tough test in Julia Görges on Saturday.

"It's either play doubles or practice for two hours, so I'd rather play doubles," Serena said of her days off from singles. "But the only difference is I'm actually getting in extra match play, and I'm really lacking match play. So I'm in a position where I need the matches."

At least until the grass-court season, Venus is the family doubles specialist. She is also the more conservative dresser, which has not always been the case at the French Open.

While Venus took to Court 7 on Friday in a patterned skirt and red halter top, Serena was back in the black bodysuit that she calls her

"Catsuit 2.0," in reference to the outfit she wore at the 2002 United States Open. The latest version has almost surpassed her resurgent tennis as the talking point of the first week at Roland Garros.

"I love the catsuit," said Andrea Petkovic, the German player who will face No. 1 Simona Halep in the third round. "I might copy her catsuit and walk with it, but probably only in New York, because that's, I guess, the only city where you can actually pull it off."

Serena, so dominant for so long and often so territorial on court, has not always been an easy champion for the tennis world to embrace. But that equation has changed, with Williams actually an underdog as she tries to come back from a very difficult childbirth at age 36.

Philippe Dehaes, the thoughtful Belgian who coaches the young Russian star Daria Kasatkina, was watching closely as the unseeded Williams came back to beat the 17th-seeded Ash Barty, a 22-year-old Australian, in three sets on Thursday evening.

"Serena has great tennis talent, but above all she has this fire," Dehaes said. "And when I watch the other young players coming up now, I just don't see it. It's the whole package with Serena: the confidence, the desire to win or more refusing to lose as if losing were an illness. I honestly didn't think she'd beat Barty, who is 17th in the world.

"But when I see Serena winning I am angry in a way," he continued, making quotation marks in the air with his fingers as he said 'angry.' "I am happy to see her win of course because I have a lot of respect for her, but I'm angry when I think of the others. I say, 'Wake up, girls. Serena is nearly 37 years old. What does it take for you to wake up?' "

A run to the title by Williams might prove just the thing. But then there are still so many hurdles and tough opponents ahead before something that crazy transpires in Paris.

For now, with Williams set to face Görges, let's appreciate the moment and a most-enduring champion's raging against any hint of dying light.

Let's enjoy the doubles, too.

So much has happened to both sisters — and the rest of us — since 1999.

For Serena Williams, a Memorable U.S. Open Final for the Wrong Reasons

BY BEN ROTHENBERG | SEPT. 9, 2018

IN THE MIDDLE of her United States Open final against Naomi Osaka at Arthur Ashe Stadium on Saturday, with a record-tying 24th Grand Slam singles title on the line, Serena Williams was standing on the court calling the chair umpire a thief.

This is not the way it was supposed to go for Williams, 36, perhaps the greatest player her sport has seen, on a night that was supposed to be a celebration of her career and her comeback to the top of tennis a year after giving birth.

After Osaka dominated the first set, another sign that this would not be a coronation for Williams came early in the second, when she received a warning for receiving help from her coach in the stands.

A few games later, Williams slammed her racket and broke it. That garnered a penalty point in Osaka's favor. Still steaming from the previous warning, Williams fumed at the chair umpire and, as tensions rose on the court and in the crowd, she received a game penalty that gave Osaka a 5-3 lead, one game from the title.

Within minutes, instead of trading blazing ground strokes with Osaka, a 20-year-old born in Japan who grew up idolizing her, Williams was having a heated conversation with the tournament referee. "There are men out here that do a lot worse," she said, "but because I'm a woman, because I'm a woman, you're going to take this away from me? That is not right."

For Williams, this was all too familiar. She has had a series of run-ins with officials at the Open, the Grand Slam event that she has won six times but that she has also been eliminated from four times in matches with contentious officiating.

Williams did not recover in time to salvage Saturday's match, which Osaka won, 6-2, 6-4. But as the boos and whistles rained down on the court during the awards ceremony, Williams resumed her role as the sport's leader, urging the fans to appreciate the first Japanese player to win a Grand Slam singles title.

"Let's give everyone the credit where credit's due and let's not boo anymore," she said to the fans.

Pam Shriver, a 1978 U.S. Open finalist who reported for ESPN during the final, said Williams's assertion that sexism had contributed to the harsh penalty was "in this day and age, a fair take."

It was unfortunate, she said, given the significance of the match that the umpire could not restore order.

"One of the main roles of an umpire is to keep order in a match, and order was lost," Shriver said. "Serena has some certain blame for it, because she couldn't let go. She felt she was wronged."

On Twitter, Billie Jean King, one of the founders of the WTA Tour, supported Williams by writing: "When a woman is emotional, she's 'hysterical' and she's penalized for it. When a man does the same, he's 'outspoken' and there are no repercussions. Thank you, @serenawilliams, for calling out this double standard."

Williams said she hoped that her taking a stand would enable women to be freer in the future.

"That I have to go through this is just an example for the next person that has emotions, and that wants to express themselves, and wants to be a strong woman," she said. "They're going to be allowed to do that because of today. Maybe it didn't work out for me, but it's going to work out for the next person."

Tournaments on the women's tour allow coaches to come onto the court during changeovers to instruct players; Williams is one of the few players who has never utilized on-court coaching. At the Open, as well as at the other Grand Slam events, coaching from the stands, verbally or by signals, is not allowed.

In a statement after the match, officials from the United States

Tennis Association explained that once the chair umpire made his rulings, they were irreversible.

Williams vigorously disputed each of the three rulings; the coaching violation seemed to be the most offensive to her. It was the first of her career.

"I don't cheat to win; I'd rather lose," she told the chair umpire, Carlos Ramos.

Williams's coach, Patrick Mouratoglou, acknowledged that he was trying to give her instructions, but said that she did not see him. Williams also seemed to indicate that she did not see the gesture that caused the violation.

Shriver and Mouratoglou pointed out that umpires typically gave an unofficial warning, not a code violation, after the first glimpse of possible coaching.

Mouratoglou said he understood Williams's distress at a ruling that she was trying to gain an illicit advantage.

"Being called a cheater, she felt even more humiliated," Mouratoglou said. "She was thinking: 'What will my daughter think of me? They are calling me a cheater.' That's how she experienced it."

Ramos, who works primarily on the men's tour, is known for being one of the strictest umpires, notably giving time violations to the slow-moving Rafael Nadal where other umpires are more lax.

"I say it with sadness, but he is an umpire who scrutinizes me more and who fixates on me more," Nadal said of Ramos after a match at the French Open last year. "He also pressured me about coaching. I have respect for him, and all I ask is for that to be reciprocated."

On Saturday, Williams repeatedly told Ramos she wanted an apology.

"For you to attack my character is something that's wrong," Williams said during a changeover. "It's wrong. You're attacking my character. Yes, you are. You owe me an apology. You will never, ever, ever be on another court of mine as long as you live. You are the liar."

She concluded, "You stole a point from me, you're a thief, too."

That remark triggered the code violation for verbal abuse, which is defined in the rule book as "a statement about an official, opponent, sponsor, spectator or other person that implies dishonesty or is derogatory, insulting or otherwise abusive."

The statement from tournament officials said that Ramos's decision on the verbal abuse — ultimately a judgment call (unlike the racket abuse, which was automatic) — "was final and not reviewable."

In her postmatch news conference, when asked if she would change anything that had happened, Williams said: "I can't sit here and say I wouldn't say he's a thief, because I thought he took a game from me. But I've seen other men call other umpires several things. I'm here fighting for women's rights and for women's equality and for all kinds of stuff. For me to say 'thief' and for him to take a game, it made me feel like it was a sexist remark. He's never taken a game from a man because they said 'thief.' "

This was not the first time in this year's tournament that officials had been called sexist. The French player Alizé Cornet received an unsportsmanlike-conduct warning for taking off her top on court after she had inadvertently put it on backward; the Open changed that rule the next day after outrage over the episode.

Williams's assertion that female players are policed more than male players is difficult to prove. At this year's Open, men have received 23 fines for code violations, compared with nine for women.

Most of the sport's infamous brats have been men, and they have often been punished for bad behavior. John McEnroe, the best-known instigator, was frequently assessed point and game penalties during his career. He was disqualified from a fourth-round match at the 1990 Australian Open after a series of outbursts.

Fabio Fognini, another serial offender, was ejected from the United States Open last year for making crude remarks in Italian about a female chair umpire during a first-round match.

For Williams, the issues are more complicated, given her history of controversy at the tournament.

In 2004, Williams lost a quarterfinal against Jennifer Capriati in large part because of a spate of erroneous overrules by the chair umpire Mariana Alves. The tournament apologized to Williams, and introduced the Hawkeye review technology the next year.

In 2009, in a semifinal against Kim Clijsters, Williams was called for a foot fault by the lineswoman Shino Tsurubuchi and responded with a threat to shove a tennis ball down Tsurubuchi's throat. Williams was given a point penalty by the chair umpire Louise Engzell, and because it was match point for Clijsters at the time, the penalty ended the match.

In 2011, in the final against Samantha Stosur, Williams celebrated what she thought was a winning shot too early, and then reacted with indignation to a hindrance call assessed by the chair umpire Eva Asderaki, calling her "a hater" and "unattractive inside." Williams lost that match, too.

But the call Saturday about illicit coaching produced a different reaction, seeming to wound Williams more than it angered her.

As she addressed the crowd in her concession speech during the trophy ceremony, Williams acknowledged her fraught track record in New York on a night when most thought she was going to be speaking about her latest landmark triumph in a sport she has ruled for nearly two decades.

"I hope to continue and play here again, but we'll see," she said with a short, knowing laugh. "It's been tough for me here, but thank you so much."

CHRISTOPHER CLAREY contributed reporting.

CHAPTER 5

Life in the Spotlight and Advocacy

Early in her career, Serena Williams also made waves with her unconventional on-court outfits, but this was only the start of her foray into fashion. She has since brought her fashion sensibilities to the runway and the general public, designing clothing collections and winning the praise of fashionistas such as Anna Wintour. She also counts numerous A-list celebrities among her friends and admirers, including Beyoncé and Meghan Markle. Williams also uses her celebrity status to speak out on social and political issues, including racism and sexism, often using social media to spread awareness of these issues.

The Tennis Balls Were White Once, Too

BY LIZ ROBBINS | SEPT. 3, 2000

EVERY GRAND SLAM awards a silver trophy and a hefty pile of green to the player who wins seven straight matches over the course of two grueling weeks. But in front of the television or from the nosebleed seats, fans become armchair umpires of what's really in and out. Their prize? Call it the Golden Hanger.

It is only one week into the United States Open at the National Tennis Center in Queens, but it's already game, set, match to Serena Williams, at least in terms of the attention paid to her clothes.

The spirit of Jerry Garcia clings to her chiseled body in the form of an electric-purple tie-dyed frock that has eclipsed even the red and yellow, thin-strapped numbers that turn her sister, Venus, into a flash of lightning trailing a rush of flying limbs.

Serena Williams has worn two variations on the mesh outfit thus far, with sneakers to match, looking like an exuberant hostess obviously pleased with her party dress. "I think it is very flattering," she said after her first-round victory.

Some fans disagree on that point, but her attire demonstrates a fashion reality: what is new is often borrowed from the past. "I just laugh when I see her, and everybody says she's the first to do that," said Billie Jean King, a tennis pioneer who, like today's players, knows that entertainment is as much a part of the game as athleticism.

When King won the "Battle of the Sexes" match against Bobby Riggs in 1973, she wore royal blue shoes to match the pattern on her white dress, created by the British-born designer Ted Tinling. "I did it for color TV," King recalled. "We didn't have color TV very long then."

Tinling was elected to the International Tennis Hall of Fame for his contributions to the evolution of women's outfits. He dressed players as modern as Monica Seles and as historic as Suzanne Lenglen (who had, in 1919, shocked Wimbledon by winning with her stockings rolled down). At Wimbledon in 1949, he designed Gertrude (Gussy) Moran's lace panties, and photographers lined the court for a glimpse.

Compared to that, the much-ogled Anna Kournikova seems tame this year, no longer baring her midriff, but wearing a sporty sleeveless shirt and short shorts. (The Open has no restrictions on color, as Wimbledon does, requiring mostly white clothing; by contract, women must display their sponsor patch on their tops.)

As Serena Williams's bold interpretation shows, women's outfits have changed greatly since the red gingham jumper Tracy Austin wore at the United States Open in 1977, which now looks like something out of the musical "Oklahoma."

Mary Pierce loved many of Austin's dresses, and Chris Evert's, too, which is why she agreed to incorporate the tennis dress into her own wardrobe in the early 1990's when Nike suggested it. At this United States Open, Pierce is back in a skirt, but she has earned points for creativity with the "elastophane" straps on her light-blue swirled top. They look like Scotch tape, but Pierce says they are very comfortable.

Comfort was the point in one of the game's first fashion statements, made by a man who died a week ago at the age of 94, Bunny Austin. In 1932, at a time when long flannel pants were de rigueur on the courts, Austin arrived at the 1932 United States Championships in shorts, his bare legs bristling before the genteel spectators.

Men's hemlines rose from there, going so short that when Stan Smith won Wimbledon in 1972 in shorts that neared his knees, other players commented. But after the short-short diehards Jimmy Connors and Boris Becker retired, the shorts crept back down. Then they got baggy, with Andre Agassi in denim and Pete Sampras apparently dressing for a backyard barbecue.

Back when men's shorts were still rising, the shirt spectrum was expanding. Starting in the late 1960's, John Newcombe, Tony Roche and six other players known as the Handsome Eight were ordered to wear bright-colored shirts to promote World Championship Tennis, the fledgling professional tour. Pros like Stan Smith and Arthur Ashe wore pastel.

These days, the men's wardrobe — like their tour, in fact — is not quite as dramatic as the women's. Gustavo Kuerten of Brazil wears bright yellow and blue to honor the national colors of his country, but he lost in the first round. The defending champion, Agassi, who favors pale gray and white in his later years, lost quietly in the second.

There is plenty of show left, though, from the baseline to the hemline. Even the fans who have already awarded the Golden Hanger know they have yet to see the best of the crosscourt backhands and rifled serves. Fans remember the champions for these images above all.

Noticed; Williamsmania Sweeps The Black A-List

BY LIZ ROBBINS | SEPT. 9, 2001

STAR JONES, the bubbly television entertainer, was more than happy to sign an autograph for a young fan this week at Arthur Ashe Stadium in Flushing Meadows, even as she was watching one of her two favorite players. "But why are you asking me?" she questioned the boy.

"Because," he answered, "I understand you know Serena."

And so it has come to pass. The stars are not coming to be seen, but flocking to tennis matches to mingle in the same aura as Venus and Serena Williams, sharers of a surname that has revolutionized tennis and rallied the African-American sports and entertainment communities. "They're starting to make tennis one of these 'you got to be there' sports," Ms. Jones said. "They have changed the way we look at tennis."

With their brash, powerful games, glistening muscles, bright tight outfits, trademark confidence and high-profile championships, the Williams sisters have an electric appeal — one that transcends race and age. "I love my girls," Ms. Jones said adoringly, adding: "Fans from one group make you popular. But fans from all groups make you a superstar."

The reason for such love, said another courtside fan, the director Spike Lee, is simple. "They can play. They got game. They got ball."

But he pointed out that black Americans especially were pulling for the sisters and explained exactly why: "They've got, you know the word?" He paused before summarizing, with a nod and a pleased smile: "Negritude."

It is not known whether Aimé Césaire, the poet from Martinique who introduced the literary concept of Negritude — consciousness and affirmation of African cultural heritage — is a tennis fan. But the large number of black celebrities attending the Open, which culminated in an all-Williams final last night, suggests that the sisters have moved to the top of their A-list.

Seen at courtside: Mary J. Blige, Paula Abdul, Vivica A. Fox and Brandy, who has been a friend of Serena Williams's for two years. The mother of the rap artist Usher asked to be in the house for Venus's quarterfinal match against Kim Clijsters. Michael Strahan of the New York Giants, as well as Allan Houston and Marcus Camby of the Knicks, all made the Williams scene, as did the rapper Jay-Z. Lil Bow Wow asked to perform at Arthur Ashe Kids Day because he knew Serena was also featured.

The actor Jamie Foxx came to Venus's postmatch news conference Tuesday afternoon and greeted her afterward with a big hug and kiss, fawning over her as if he were her long-lost friend. Venus, though a bit taken aback at his enthusiasm, was polite and jokingly apologized for her poor showing in his charity basketball tournament a couple of years ago. It's not her game, really, she said. Foxx clearly did not mind.

Of course, the Williamses have been demonstrating their drawing power among black celebrities at tournaments all year. Shaquille O'Neal and Kobe Bryant of the Lakers have requested, separately, to watch the sisters. (Mr. O'Neal even suggested in a radio interview that he had been intimate with Venus Williams — which she vehemently denied.) Diana Ross went to San Diego this summer just to see Venus play.

Venus came into the United States Open the defending champion and the reigning two-time Wimbledon champion, having won two other tour titles this summer. She is 21; Serena is 19. They are already multimillionaires. Last month they were on the cover of Time magazine.

Their metamorphosis from giggly, braces-clad teenagers, coached by their father, Richard, on the cracked courts of Compton, Calif., has paralleled the rise of another superstar.

"They have done for tennis, to some degree at least, that which Tiger Woods did for golf," said David N. Dinkins, the former New York mayor, who is on the board of the United States Tennis Association. "People who before had no interest in the sport, now have it. I think they clearly have an appeal. Go back to when they dared to be different. They were wearing beads. They have such confidence in their own ability."

Mr. Lee, too, acknowledges this Tigerizing effect. "They have both brought style to tennis, athleticism," he said. "None of those golfers worked out until Tiger did; now they have got to do everything he does just to keep up with him. Look at the way Venus and Serena look. I don't even know if they work out. They might just be like that. It's great."

"In sports, you need stars," he continued. "And they have that star presence, the way they look, the way they dress, the way they emote on the court. And it makes good drama. And lots of the other players don't like that. A lot of times you have that dislike, and that's O.K."

And Zina Garrison, for one, finds the sisters' easygoing attitude toward fame "really amazing." Ms. Garrison, the last black woman in a major final before the Williamses, and a mentor of Serena's, remembers going to visit her after a match in Palm Springs.

"All these people, like groupies, were waiting for her outside the locker room," she said. "I never saw that when I was playing. They're attracting a new wave of kids. I think it's more and more the fact that they are on the covers of all kinds of magazines. They are entertainers."

Entertainers of entertainers, it seems. "What's so great is that they're so young," Mr. Lee said. "And they have got their whole life in front of them."

They're Young. They're Sexy. They're Targets.

BY SELENA ROBERTS | JULY 1, 2002

ON THE SLICK PAGES of the new official magazine for the women's tennis tour, there are the ubiquitous images of Anna Kournikova in different stages of a hair toss, snapshots of the curvaceous sports cars preferred by the top stars and a glimpse of the luxury hotels frequented by the players on the road.

On one page, Venus and Serena Williams are in a paparazzi shot dressed in slinky evening wear. On the next, a player on a reprinted poster has her back to the camera, lifting her skirt while grabbing her own bare bottom. There are player tips on buying diamonds, moisturizers and salt scrubs, but no tips on shot selection, no discussions on strategy.

"A lot has changed," said Monica Seles, a witness to the evolution of the sport who is now in her 15th year on the WTA Tour. "Now, players are a lot more worried about image. Before, it was about playing tennis. I think there is a lot more competition about making sure you look good and your image fits a certain thing out there. There's a lot more pressure in that sense."

There is nothing subtle about the Tour's approach to marketing its sport. The unveiling of the Tour magazine at Harrods a week ago, a day before Wimbledon began, only underscores the unabashed use of sex appeal to broaden the reach of women's tennis. The approach has been going on for several years.

Even critics concede the controversial blueprint has worked to increase the sport's fan base, lift prize money and raise television ratings beyond those of the men's game. But as exposure has increased, as more players pout into the cameras and as more chat rooms form on the Internet, there is a downside to this spike in global celebrity: privacy concerns, security issues and a rise in what one top-10 player referred to as "the creep factor" in describing obsessive fans.

Several players have had brushes with stalkers over the past few years, including, most recently, Serena Williams. This year, a German man began shadowing her at events, sending her inappropriate e-mail messages and requesting a rendezvous. At the Italian Open in May, he was arrested and later released.

Pictures of her stalker have been distributed to security personnel at all Tour events, including the officials at Wimbledon. Amid the uneasiness of the situation, and with her run to a possible berth in the finals expected to unfold this week, Williams has hired a bodyguard for peace of mind.

"I'm not afraid, but I'm cautious," she said. "It might be scary sometimes, but at the end, I have to live my life. As popularity grows, there is a price you pay. But I'd prefer to be a successful person than turn away from that because it has a big personal price tag on it.

"I'm not playing tennis for the popularity or the money — when you're young you don't think of that. I play because I enjoy it. You can't complain about it. This is the life I've chosen."

Williams is not isolated in her predicament. A year ago, Martina Hingis sat on the witness stand in a Miami courtroom to testify against Dubravko Rajcevic, a 46-year-old Croatian-born engineer who stalked her for 20 months after he saw her on television. He sent Hingis dozens of love letters, followed her at events and showed up at her Zurich home.

Through the iron gates of her house, Hingis said she told Rajcevic to get out of her life, but that he "told me we were engaged." In her testimony, she added that she was "frightened that his obsession and love for me might turn into aggression and hate."

Rajcevic was sentenced to two years in prison.

Tour officials are aware of how vulnerable their players are. The stars are in their teens and early 20's, but the new chief executive of the Tour, Kevin Wulff, an executive at Nike until last fall, has no reservations about the way the stars are marketed for public consumption.

"The brighter the star shines, the likelier it is for a fan, because exposure is so great, to fall into that pattern," he said of obsessive behavior. "Our stars are shining quite bright right now.

"We have athletes who appeal to urban consumers and hip-hop. We have athletes who are Prada, you know, very high fashion. We have athletes who are very casual end — Gap-ish. I think everything has always been in good taste. Over all, we're pleased with how the players handle themselves off the court. It's the nature of who they are. They shouldn't be ashamed of it."

Wulff said security was a priority. The Tour consults with an American-based security firm and has plainclothes and visible guards at every Tour event. But when the players travel, they are on their own to deal with fame.

"You can be in a store, trying on clothes," said Kim Clijsters, a 19-year-old, top-five player from Belgium. "Everyone knows you."

The popularity indexes reflect the attention. In 1997, the Tour's attendance total was 3.5 million. It jumped to 4.27 million in 2001. Last year, the women broke TV ratings records, led by the first prime-time final, between Venus and Serena Williams at the United States Open. The 6.8 rating almost doubled the number for the Notre Dame-Nebraska college football telecast on a competing network.

The prize money on the women's Tour has also boomed, leaping from a total of $25.5 million in 1992 to $51.7 million this year. At the end of the 2001 season, four players — Venus and Serena Williams, Jennifer Capriati and Lindsay Davenport — had earned more than $2 million each.

Off the court, the rewards can be even more lucrative. On Forbes magazine's 2002 Celebrity 100 list, a composite of star power and earnings, Venus Williams was No. 60, with an income of $11 million, and Serena Williams was No. 72 ($8 million). Kournikova, Hingis and Capriati also made the list.

A less exact measure of popularity is on Web searches. An entry on Shaquille O'Neal produced 122,000 results, while Venus Williams turned up 255,000.

Of these links, many are message boards. Chat rooms are generally harmless, but some fans are sexually explicit in their opinions of certain female players. On rare occasions, a fan will leave cyberspace and enter a player's personal space.

"As more people want to get close, you're going to get more incidents," said Chris De Maria, vice president of the Tour's communications. "Ninety-nine percent of the fans just want an autograph, and there is about 1 percent who could be dangerous."

Most players are not overly concerned about the risks of celebrity. Only a few Tour stars resist the opportunity to sell their image. Capriati is one of them. After burning out on exposure during her teens, she prefers her privacy, often turning down chances to pitch products and appear on talk shows.

The fame and outside income are bait for other players, though some complain when their privacy is violated. Indulging in a publicity opportunity, Jelena Dokic is scheduled to be part of a GQ photo spread, but she bristled last week during a news conference when asked if she was dating the Formula 1 driver Enrique Benoldi.

"If I wasn't a tennis player, you wouldn't be talking to me right now," Dokic said. "So why don't you think of a question that is your business, and you can ask me that."

Player ambivalence toward fame is widespread. Many crave the glamour and lifestyle, but there is an unsettling downside.

"Life is a trade-off," said Billie Jean King, a founder of the Tour who knew promotion was the key to equal pay and success with the men's Tour. "Our players, they're entertainers first. They just happen to be in sports. Is it comfortable? Absolutely not. Is it tough? Yeah, but you cannot have everything."

Williamses Aren't Outsiders, But They're Still Different

BY SELENA ROBERTS | AUG. 25, 2002

THE INVITATION-ONLY tennis society no longer stares at Venus and Serena Williams as if they were two gate-crashers who just swiped through the icing of the petit fours.

Over the past five years, Venus and Serena have taken over the establishment and made it their own with a bold style and haymaker swings never before witnessed in the sport. As they have become less of a curiosity and more of a fixture on the scene, it is easy to forget how Venus and Serena would be folk-tale characters if not for their flesh and bone, how the passage of two African-American sisters from the inner city to worldwide fame would be a fantasy if it weren't so real.

It is easy to get lost in the victories that have left Serena No. 1 and Venus No. 2 and forget their journey along the way to winning 7 of the last 11 majors. Venus has four and Serena has three as they arrive at the United States Open this week.

"I can compare it to if Tiger Woods had a brother who was No. 2 in golf," said Mary Carillo, a former player who is a CBS analyst. "That is basically what Venus and Serena have done. It's one of those remarkable stories. It's so improbable that it almost seems impossible."

But despite the Woodslike social impact the sisters have made as minority success stories and the similar backgrounds the athletes share as products of public parks, despite the sisters' unmatched dominance in their sport and their charismatic star quality, Venus and Serena are not afforded the same reverence from their peers, total embrace from fans or margin for human error that Tiger Woods has enjoyed.

He can curse on the golf course, duck uncomfortable issues, receive a reported $60 million a year to pitch corporate products and withdraw from events with little backlash. It is not the same for Venus and Serena. While the sisters have disarmed many of their critics by maturing into gracious champions, they are still scrutinized on a harsh level by jealous peers and by fans who seem to resent two powerful black women leading change.

While Venus and Serena are sports icons, transcending tennis as cover subjects on magazines like Time, according to Forbes's Celebrity 100 list for 2002, they are also well behind the male stars in pay, a disparity of a different sort.

"I live comfortably; I'm grateful and I'm not a greedy person," Venus Williams said in an interview last week. "Nowadays, in this market, you have to be an athlete who is superspecial, and you have to win all the time.

"But the thing is, women are historically paid less than men. That's changing, but that's a factor that plays into it."

According to the Forbes list, Venus's annual income is $11 million, while Serena's is $8 million. Three years ago, Venus signed a $40 million deal with Reebok for five years, and Serena could approach those figures with a coming shoe deal, with suitors like Nike vying to sign her away from Puma.

As well as Venus and Serena have done — and they are the first to appreciate it — their income is still in the same bracket as that of players like Martina Hingis and Jennifer Capriati. In contrast, Andre Agassi's income is listed at $18.5 million. Ten years ago, Jim Courier, the No. 1 player, had an income reported at $9 million a year.

"Perceptions about men and women are different," said Bob Williams, president of Burns Sports and Celebrities. "But there is a great potential for Venus and Serena to create change and close that gap in how women athletes are viewed.

"When the physical skills are close to a man's skills, that's when you'll see other women's sports take off like women's tennis has. In basketball, it's too big of a difference. But Venus and Serena play above the rim in their own way. When you see them, there doesn't seem like a lot of difference between how they play and the men."

While Venus and Serena have a mannerly approach to tennis — they refrain from expletives and do not bicker with umpires — their muscle is unwelcome to some fans.

Last month, a Wimbledon cabdriver underscored one slice of public opinion when he told a carful of reporters that he believed the strength of Venus and Serena was "unnatural" and "unfair." He said he longed for the days when women played a "feminine" game.

Boring: that is how players like Justine Henin have labeled the matchups between Venus and Serena. Phony: that's how Jennifer Capriati views Venus and Serena's rise to No. 1 and No. 2. Fixed: that's how Amélie Mauresmo sees the showdowns between the sisters.

Jelena Dokic, ranked No. 4, said, "I think tennis, for me, was more exciting 5 or 10 years ago than it is right now."

Martina Navratilova disagrees. Like many, she watched Serena take Wimbledon from Venus in a match of top quality and unprecedented might. "I think people need to check where they are coming from with those kinds of comments," she said. "These are two good athletes going at it, and I think they are great for the game."

Where is the negativity coming from? Tennis officials have privately suggested theories over the past few months: the culture of the teenage-based sport is innately immature (everyone is picked apart); the image of two strong-willed black women is still viewed as a threat to parts of society (code for racism).

Above it all, Venus and Serena have never complained, never accused.

"You have to be satisfied with you and who you are," Serena said after her Wimbledon title. "Venus and I have learned that we're satisfied and we're happy with us. We don't have any problem with anyone because you have to be happy with the person inside. When you're a little bitter and a little angry, then you're going to become resentful. Instead of becoming resentful, you should go do something about it."

Venus and Serena took their image into their own hands after one important turning point 18 months ago in Indian Wells, Calif. Venus pulled out of a match with Serena four minutes before their semifinal.

The timing was terrible for obvious and not-so-obvious reasons: that same week, a supermarket tabloid reported that their father, Richard Williams, had fixed their semifinal match at Wimbledon a year earlier.

Unable to dissociate themselves from their controversial father until recently, the family took a painful hit in Indian Wells. As Venus and her father made their way down the steps to watch Serena play Kim Clijsters in the final, a cascade of boos drenched them, a reaction Richard Williams later labeled as racist. The fans also took their hostility out on Serena, actually cheering on her double faults.

At the time, Agassi had a prescient response to the situation, saying Venus and Serena should take the controversy as an opportunity to "make assessments and judgments as to how you want things to go in the future, to realize that those things are in your control."

Woods isn't asked to apologize for withdrawals. Basketball stars, baseball icons and men on the tennis tour bail out of games, matches and events on a regular basis.

But Serena and Venus have come to terms with the scrutiny placed on them. Learning from Indian Wells, Serena withdrew from a tournament in Montreal two weeks ago but faced the crowd of 11,000 and voiced an apology in nearly flawless French.

They cheered her effort. Crisis averted. Another step in responsibility.

"You get a few blowups like Indian Wells," Tracy Austin said, "and you start to learn. I think they have matured. And I've got to say, it's tough to mature in front of the whole world."

Once seen as aloof, Venus and Serena Williams are known to reach out to players who are injured. Once viewed as arrogant, they have learned to credit their opponents.

"When I was younger, I didn't always compliment my opponent," Venus said. "When I lost a match, I'd just say, 'I think I played bad.' It's how you handle things."

Venus continued by admitting: "But really, I still believe that I'm the best, and I'm going to be top dog.

"I don't know why anyone would be offended by that, because, to be honest, they should be thinking they're the best, too. I know I've heard other players say, 'I thought I'd never be here,' but that's not how I felt. When I was younger, my mom and dad said, 'You're going to be there,' so of course, you believe them. I guess if you look back, they brainwashed me to think I was the best."

If you look back, Venus and Serena have come a long way in public opinion, but through little fault of their own, they have miles left to go.

Shopping With: Serena Williams; Game, Set, Dress Me In Leather

BY GINIA BELLAFANTE | OCT. 17, 1999

UNTIL NOT LONG AGO, the single greatest contribution made by an American female athlete to the history of style was that spinning plate of a haircut from the skater Dorothy Hamill — the one that for a few minutes in the 1970's changed the look of third-grade suburbanites.

The arrival of Serena and Venus Williams onto tennis courts is happily reshaping that legacy. With their colorful hair beads, jeweled wrists and tennis skirts that look as though they're on their way to a night of caipirinha-drinking with Marc Anthony, rather than an afternoon of pummeling Martina Hingis, the Williams sisters have become more than racquet-sport prodigies; they're muses, budding fashion divas in the minds of some.

Last week, at the ready-to-wear shows in Paris, the avant-garde designer Jeremy Scott turned out little dresses he said were inspired by the sisters. Last year, the young women, who if stacked on top of each other would stand over 12 feet tall, appeared in Vogue wearing gowns by Carolina Herrera. The Vogue editor Andre Leon Talley, a fan of the sisters' court style ("They burned tennis whites!" he said), recently described the photo this way: "I thought it was the second coming."

That may seem a bit extreme, except that in the world of at least one of the sisters — Serena — clothes shopping suggests a religious experience with all the fervor and devotion.

Ms. Williams, now 18, won the United States Open championship last month. Last week, she was in town to promote the Chase Championships, a tennis tournament in which she will play, beginning Nov. 15, and she seized on the chance to spend time at Saks Fifth Avenue. She did not shop alone; there was an entourage, including her mother, Brandi Williams; a representative from the World Tennis Association and a publicity agent.

In a room reserved for V.I.P. customers on the fifth floor, personal shoppers had selected 12 outfits for Ms. Williams's inspection, along with five wraps (one resembling a neon comforter), three pairs of shoes and more than 15 little handbags, which seemed even more diminutive in the presence of the broad, unwaifish athlete. Nanette DiFalco, one of the personal shoppers, said she'd chosen the clothes with the likes and dislikes of a typical 18 year old in mind. "We stayed away from anything that looked athletic because of endorsement deals," she added. When she competes, Ms. Williams is dressed exclusively by Puma.

Ms. Williams was wearing black bell-bottoms, a leather jacket and a pair of red platforms belonging to her sister Venus. She'd bought the leather jacket during a tournament in Germany. "Was it Stuttgart or Munich?" she asked her mother. It turned out to be Stuttgart, where she'd also bought two other leather jackets, a pair of leather pants and a leather hat.

Perhaps today would be the day she'd counterbalance that spree with a few things containing no animal pelts.

"This is a French seam," Ms. Williams said knowingly, as she stroked and ogled a pink DKNY top with rhinestone chains for straps. "I'm in design school," she added, and indeed, after winning the Open, Ms. Williams enrolled in the Art Institute of Florida, where she is taking classes in drawing, sewing and psychology.

Ms. Williams has a fashion diva's penchant for proclamation. Going through the selections — two skirts, some rubberized pants, more DKNY tops, a Vivienne Tam knit sequined skirt and sweater, some white denim — she rattled off her thoughts on style like a Diana Vreeland with menacing calves. "Purple is in," she announced. Gravitating toward the accessories table, she said: "I love bags! I think you can really express yourself with a bag. Flat bags are in!" But she didn't seem to want the flat bag with floral applique from Patch. "The problem with a flat bag is you put too much in it, and then it ruins the whole purpose," she said.

She also rejected a pair of white pants from Helmut Lang that were embellished with side pockets and Velcro straps. "I wouldn't get into these pants," Ms. Williams said. "There's just too much going on here."

In the end, like legions of adolescents before her, Ms. Williams could not resist the rebellious pull of leather. She tried on a mini leather wrap skirt that reversed to pony skin on the flip side. The label wasn't as posh as Helmut Lang's — Elements by Vakko — but it was more to Ms. Williams's taste. She paired it with a pink sleeveless turtleneck from DKNY. And where, one wondered, might she wear such an ensemble?

"I could go to school in it," she said, sizing herself up in a mirror. "Ricky Martin has a concert coming up."

Ms. Williams described the evolution of her off-court dress code. "I started with Bebe, and then I went on to BCBG and then Max Mara," she said. "I really like Max Mara." But there was nothing from any of those manufacturers lined up for her at Saks. "I have a $1,400 shirt from Dolce & Gabbana," she noted. "They're too expensive."

After trying on the rubberized pants and Vivienne Tam knits and deeming them not quite right, the young champion settled on the leather mini and DKNY top. She also picked out a silver Kate Spade purse and silver DKNY sandals. Saks offered her a gift of a pink pashmina shawl, but Ms. Williams wasn't quite sure what pashmina was.

Her total purchases came to $798.85 — closer to those of a Long Island teen-ager than to the damage a Miller sister might have done during a retail excursion. And she paid for it the way an average teen-ager would, too, using her mother's credit card.

Her U.S. Open Loss Behind Her, Serena Williams Turns to Fashion

BY VALERIYA SAFRONOVA | SEPT. 13, 2016

LAST MONDAY, JUST DAYS after losing her No. 1 ranking after a defeat to Karolina Pliskova in the United States Open semifinals, Serena Williams, clad in a shimmering transparent dress of her own design, presented her latest collection for HSN, the shopping network.

The stress of losing a big match while preparing for a runway show in the middle of New York Fashion Week wasn't apparent.

"Mostly, it's easy to balance," Ms. Williams said, explaining that on days when she didn't have to play, she went over "tons of looks," and that the team she works with knows not to bother her during a tournament. "I'm usually the one reaching out, asking questions."

The line, which included 42 pieces ranging in price from under $30

DANNY GHITIS FOR THE NEW YORK TIMES

The front row included Anna Wintour, who provides feedback to Ms. Williams after every show.

LIFE IN THE SPOTLIGHT AND ADVOCACY   **173**

to nearly $700, was immediately available on HSN.com, making it yet another example of the see-now, buy-now trend at fashion week.

Backstage after the show, Tommy Hilfiger, who similarly offered a ready-to-buy collection last Friday, praised Ms. Williams's designs and their immediate availability for purchase. "It's the way of the world," he said. "We've got to go there."

It was Ms. Williams's third collection for HSN, and the focus was on the power of women. As models slowly strode down the runway, "Pray You Catch Me," from Beyoncé's latest album, "Lemonade," boomed from the speakers, along with Ms. Williams's voice, reading a poem she wrote after competing at Wimbledon and at the Olympics that included lines like "All women are her inspirations/She is unapologetically bold and beautiful."

"We do so much," Ms. Williams said after the show. "We birth, we sit in boardrooms, we do everything. We're not praised enough. I want to praise every woman."

Fittingly, her front row included a slew of accomplished women: her sister Venus, who has her own clothing line called EleVen; the singer Ciara; the fashion icon Iris Apfel; her friend and fellow tennis player Caroline Wozniacki; and the Vogue editor Anna Wintour. Serena attributed her, and Venus's, love of fashion to another significant female figure: their mother. "When I was younger, she had us sewing, making things," Serena said.

Has Ms. Wintour's discerning presence become easier to handle over several seasons? Kind of. "She has such high standards," Serena Williams said. "It definitely makes it stressful, but also we're such good friends." She noted that Ms. Wintour provides feedback after every show. "In my job, I take feedback every day, so I'm really good at it," Ms. Williams said. "I don't want to hear a positive, I want to hear what I can do better."

The interplay between her sport and her work in fashion doesn't end there. "This year, I don't feel like it's all that different from what I do," she said about designing the line. "It takes a lot of focus, it takes a lot of dedication, it takes a lot of work."

Serena Williams Gives Birth to a Baby Girl

BY MATT STEVENS | SEPT. 1, 2017

SERENA WILLIAMS HAS given birth to a girl, according to the United States Open's official Twitter account and her coach.

The highly anticipated announcement came late Friday afternoon as Serena's sister Venus Williams romped over another opponent and into the fourth round of the major tennis tournament in Flushing, Queens.

Asked just before her match on Friday about reports of Serena having given birth and about becoming an aunt, Venus Williams told ESPN's Pam Shriver she was "super excited," adding, "Words can't describe."

She then proceeded to defeat Maria Sakkari of Greece in straight sets, 6-3, 6-4. Afterward, she sidestepped questions about the birth of her niece, saying: "I'm definitely available to answer questions about tennis. That's all right now."

Serena Williams, 35, has not played a match since winning her 23rd Grand Slam singles title at the Australian Open on Jan. 28. It was later discovered that she had been close to two months pregnant at the time, after a photograph was posted on the tennis superstar's Snapchat story on April 19 that showed her posing sideways in a yellow bathing suit with what looked like a baby bump. The image, which appeared to have been taken in a mirror, was captioned "20 weeks" and was later deleted.

After a wild day of speculation, Williams confirmed she was pregnant. She had unexpectedly announced her engagement to Alexis Ohanian, a businessman and the co-founder of Reddit, months earlier, in December.

A spokeswoman for Williams, Kelly Bush Novak, previously told The New York Times that although Serena would miss the rest of the 2017 season, she intended to return to the circuit in 2018.

In an email late Friday, Novak said she could not confirm any reports of Williams having given birth. Williams's agent, Jill Smoller, did not immediately respond to an email from The Times.

But her coach, Patrick Mouratoglou, did congratulate the new mother on Twitter.

"I wish you a speedy recovery," Mouratoglou wrote, adding, "we have a lot of work ahead of us."

NAILA-JEAN MEYERS contributed reporting.

For Serena Williams, Childbirth Was a Harrowing Ordeal. She's Not Alone.

BY MAYA SALAM | JAN. 11, 2018

NOT EVEN THE TENNIS dynamo Serena Williams is immune from the complications and challenges new mothers face during and after childbirth.

In a Vogue cover story published online on Wednesday, Ms. Williams, who holds 23 Grand Slam titles — some call her a superhero, others a queen — shared her agonizing postnatal experience, including an episode in which hospital employees did not act on her concern that she was experiencing a pulmonary embolism, a sudden blockage of an artery in the lung by a blood clot. She is prone to such clots, a condition that nearly killed her in 2011.

"Serena lives in fear of blood clots," the Vogue article said.

On Sept. 2, the day after giving birth to her daughter via cesarean section, Ms. Williams was having trouble breathing and "immediately assumed she was having another pulmonary embolism," the article says.

She alerted a nurse to what she felt was happening in her body and asked for a CT scan and a blood thinner, but the nurse suggested that pain medication had perhaps left Ms. Williams confused, according to Vogue. Ms. Williams insisted, but a doctor instead performed an ultrasound of her legs.

"I was like, a Doppler? I told you, I need a CT scan and a heparin drip," Ms. Williams, 36, said she told the medical team.

When the ultrasound revealed nothing, she underwent a CT scan, which showed several small blood clots in her lungs. She was immediately put on the heparin drip. "I was like, listen to Dr. Williams!" she told the doctors.

A spokeswoman for Ms. Williams declined to comment beyond the Vogue article.

The need to ensure that medical professionals are responsive to new mothers' concerns has gained attention in recent years. The "Stop. Look. Listen!" campaign, for example, which was introduced in 2012, aims to empower women to report pregnancy-related medical issues and to increase awareness and responsiveness among health care practitioners.

About 700 women die each year in the United States as a result of pregnancy or delivery complications, according to the Centers for Disease Control and Prevention. Complications affect more than 50,000 women annually. And the risk of pregnancy-related death is three to four times as high for black women as it is for white women, the C.D.C. says.

Even more troubling, the numbers have increased steadily from 7.2 deaths per 100,000 live births in 1987 to a high of 17.8 deaths per 100,000 live births in 2009 and 2011, according to the C.D.C.

The "Stop. Look. Listen!" campaign — a collaboration between the Tara Hansen Foundation and the Robert Wood Johnson Medical School at Rutgers — was developed to honor the life of Tara Hansen, a young mother who was sent home after delivery despite raising concerns about how she felt. She died six days later from an undiagnosed infection.

The campaign has prompted New Jersey to designate Jan. 23 as Maternal Health Awareness Day, the first state to designate a day to the cause.

For Ms. Williams, the clots were only the beginning of her complications. In the days after she gave birth, bouts of severe coughing — a result of the embolism — caused her C-section wound to open. She returned to surgery, during which doctors found a large hematoma, a collection of blood outside of the blood vessels, in her abdomen. She was then back in the operating room for a procedure to help prevent more clots from dislodging and traveling to her lungs.

Ms. Williams was bedridden for her first six weeks of motherhood.

Life-threatening complications in the delivery room, and during recovery, are all too common — particularly for black and Hispanic women.

A series last year by the nonprofit investigative journalism organization ProPublica and NPR explored why black women disproportionately suffer complications around pregnancy and childbirth.

ProPublica analyzed how different medical facilities in New York, Illinois and Florida treated women who experienced hemorrhages during childbirth. It found, as has other research, that women who hemorrhage at disproportionately black-serving hospitals are significantly more likely to experience severe complications like birth-related embolisms and emergency hysterectomies.

Poverty, access to care, culture, communication and decision-making all contribute to disparities, Dr. Elizabeth Howell, professor and director of the Women's Health Research Institute at the Icahn School of Medicine in New York, said on Wednesday. Still, the problem is often attributed incorrectly solely to poverty, she said.

"Everyone always wants to say that it's just about access to care and it's just about insurance, but that alone doesn't explain it," said Dr. Howell, whose research focuses on quality of care and racial and ethnic disparities in maternal and child health.

Dr. Howell and ProPublica both pointed to a 2016 analysis that found that black college-educated mothers who gave birth in New York City hospitals were more likely to suffer severe complications during pregnancy and childbirth than uneducated white women.

New York City is increasingly confronting the role that racism plays in health outcomes, Dr. Howell said. "There's more and more emphasis to thinking about the ways bias shapes the way we hear our patients," she said.

In This Sports Gender Gap, Men Fall Short

OPINION | BY WILL LEITCH | SEPT. 15, 2017

THE ELECTRIC TALENT Sloane Stephens, a player just now coming into her own after having her career nearly wrecked by injuries, won the U.S. Open women's tournament last week. But let's not kid ourselves: The real winner of this year's tournament was Serena Williams.

More specifically, Serena Williams's Instagram. From the shots of her baby shower to her glorious pregnant belly and finally an adorable shot of mother and child dozing together, Williams owned the Open. The only tennis story bigger this entire year was a seven-months-pregnant Williams smashing backhands in a video posted during Wimbledon. (Pity her poor sister, Venus: She couldn't even enjoy her own run to the Wimbledon finals without having announcers tell us how inspired she must be by Serena's impending motherhood.)

Surely, this is a step forward from years past, when female athletes had to end their careers for childbirth or were discouraged from playing when pregnant. Motherhood is now even part of female athletes' heartwarming hero narratives, like Kim Clijsters and Lindsay Davenport in tennis, and the married W.N.B.A. players DeWanna Bonner and Candice Dupree, who are raising twin daughters together despite being on different teams.

In this area — the recognition of a full life off the playing field, the acceptance that our athletes don't materialize out of thin air when they step on the field — male athletes fall short of their female counterparts. They remain stat-generating robots who exist solely to make our teams win: Their off-field lives aren't just irrelevant to us, they're annoying distractions from what really matters.

Colin Kaepernick's protest and subsequent blackballing by the N.F.L. is the most high-profile example. But our insistence that male athletes keep their lives to themselves isn't limited to their political views. Every time a male athlete takes a few days off for the birth of his child, he's inevitably showered with "Where are his priorities?" complaints from fans and sports columnists. ("If they choose not to plan their nine-month family expansion activities to coincide with the eight months per year when their work activities don't entail playing games that count, why should their teams suffer the consequences?" Mike Florio at NCB wrote, succinctly summing up the mind-set in 2012.)

Players who have taken time off to deal with mental health problems are seen as weak or somehow not "focused" enough to overcome them. "To show weakness, we're told in sports, is to deserve shame," the former tennis star Mardy Fish, who withdrew from a 2012 U.S. Open match against Roger Federer because of anxiety, told USA Today.

Emotional states in male athletes can even be mostly ignored or given more "comfortable" explanations. Stephen Piscotty, a right fielder for my beloved St. Louis Cardinals, has had a disappointing year at the plate. A logical reason for this might be that early in the season his mother was told she had A.L.S. But Piscotty's struggles have not been attributed to that. Instead, "his timing is off" or "he's just having one of those years" is the preferred nomenclature.

And compare, say, Novak Djokovic and Venus Williams. Djokovic, one of the best tennis players of all time, has had the worst year of his career, falling below No. 2 in the rankings for the first time since 2011 and prompting John McEnroe to question his desire. He left the tour in July to rest his elbow and "spend quality time" with his family.

We've grown accustomed to dismissing that as news release talk, but it turned out that his wife had their second child at the beginning of September. Few even knew she was pregnant, or even thought to ask. Surely this had something to do with Djokovic's year?

At the U.S. Open, commentators kept telling me that Venus Williams was playing great tennis because she was inspired by her sister's having a child. I think she was playing at that level because she's one of the greatest athletes on the planet and has the competitive streak to match.

When I hear a commentator note that a male athlete is affected in any possible way by his sister's having a child somewhere thousands of miles away, it will be a first. This disparity is ultimately infantilizing of female athletes, patting them on the head for off-field stories, as if their on-court accomplishments aren't enough. And while we can't stop talking about Venus Williams's off-court life, we rarely think to ask about Novak Djokovic's.

We'd rather our male athletes not have emotional lives, but if they have to have them, we'd rather not know about it.

Perhaps it's indicative of a larger need to pretend that sports are somehow separate from real life, as if our athletes have no interior lives but simply appear when we as sports fans beckon them. Why is it more pronounced for male athletes than female athletes? It might be because there are (slightly) more male sports fans than female sports fans — 66 percent of men are sports fans, 51 percent of women, in a 2015 Gallup poll — and, well, male sports fans usually watch more male athletes than female athletes. The more sports you watch, the less perspective you have, and the more likely you are to see an athlete more as a stat producer (or a key producer for your team, or the guy likely to win you gambling money) than as a human being. Women are allowed to have off-field lives that affect their on-field ones because male fans simply care about those sports less.

But there is much evidence that that is changing: Women's tennis television ratings are often better than men's, the United States women's soccer team got the highest ratings in American soccer history in 2015, and the W.N.B.A. finals notched their highest ratings last year. Women's sports are more popular than they have ever been, and that growth continues exponentially.

Which points to a potential evolution in attitudes. It's not difficult to imagine a time when this odd condescension ends and male sports fans are just as unreasonable about Serena Williams's taking time off to have a child as they are when a male athlete does the same for his child's birth. Don't mess up their fantasy tennis teams, Serena. Progress expresses itself in the strangest ways sometimes.

WILL LEITCH is a senior writer for Sports on Earth, a contributing editor for New York magazine and the founder of Deadspin.

'I Won't Be Silent': Serena Williams on the Fear of Driving While Black

BY CHRISTINE HAUSER | SEPT. 28, 2016

IT MAY SEEM mundane: having a relative drive you around to do errands.

But to the tennis champion Serena Williams, a decision to let her 18-year-old nephew drive her to meetings so that she could safely use her phone in the car filled her with misgivings that go to the heart of the national discourse on race and policing.

In a social media post on Tuesday, Ms. Williams described how spotting a police officer on the side of the road during her ride with a young black man at the wheel inspired thoughts of life and death.

"I quickly checked to see if he was obliging by the speed limit," Ms. Williams wrote on her public Facebook page. "I remembered that horrible video of the woman in the car when a cop shot her boyfriend.

"All of this went through my mind in a matter of seconds," she wrote. "I even regretted not driving myself. I would never forgive myself if something happened to my nephew."

The "woman in the car" was mostly likely a reference to the girlfriend of Philando Castile, a 32-year-old school cafeteria worker who was at the wheel when he was pulled over in July by a Hispanic police officer in a Minnesota suburb, ostensibly for a cracked taillight. He was shot and killed while reaching for his identification.

His girlfriend, Diamond Reynolds, who was at his side while her young daughter sat in the back seat, posted a video of the harrowing encounter on Facebook Live.

Mr. Castile had been pulled over by the police in the Minneapolis-St. Paul region at least 49 times in a 13-year span, often for minor infractions: turning into a parking lot without signaling; failing to repair a broken seatbelt; driving at night with an unlit license plate; driving with tinted windows.

His death came amid a period of violent protests after the police killings of black men across the nation and counterattacks that saw gunmen take the lives of officers in Dallas and Baton Rouge, La. On Tuesday, the fatal police shooting of a black man in El Cajon, Calif., who the authorities said had pointed an object at officers, was the latest flash point.

As a high-profile athlete, Ms. Williams used the weight of her celebrity to convey the despair that has gripped many black Americans after multiple police killings, most of them men. Her post also highlighted the awareness of black Americans that they are often regarded with suspicion by the authorities during everyday activities.

The cognizance, which many say is nothing new but is being talked about more frequently because of the national discussion on police shootings, has bred movements like Black Lives Matter and hashtag trends like #shoppingwhileblack.

Research has shown that black Americans are more likely to be stopped by the police than whites and are more likely to be touched, handcuffed, pushed to the ground or pepper-sprayed by an officer after being stopped.

It is a trend underscored by frequency and longevity, activists say. Back in 2009, when the well-known Harvard professor Henry Louis Gates Jr. was confronted by a Cambridge, Mass., police officer while trying to open his jammed front door, it spurred a national discussion of racial profiling and a White House "beer summit," in which President Obama invited Mr. Gates and the officer to discuss the encounter.

The roster of black victims since then has included Michael Brown, Eric Garner, Sandra Bland, Keith Scott, Tamir Rice.

The awareness that young black people in particular must be given extra coaching to avoid seeming suspicious while going about their daily lives is a concern of parents, educators and activists. Last month, for example, a 15-year-old black girl who collided with a car while riding a bicycle in Maryland was handcuffed and pepper sprayed by the police as they tried to take her into custody.

On Monday, the N.B.A. star LeBron James said that his son would start driving his own car in four years, but that he was afraid for him already. (A New York Times examination of traffic stops and arrests in Greensboro, N.C., in 2013, for example, showed officers pulled over African-American drivers at a rate far out of proportion with their share of the local driving population.)

"It's a scary thought right now to think if my son gets pulled over, and you tell your kids if you just [comply] and you just listen to the police that they will be respectful and things will work itself out," he said, according to ABC News.

He added that he was "not that confident that things are going to go well and that my son is going to return home."

The N.F.L. quarterback Colin Kaepernick, who has been vociferously criticized for protesting racial injustice by taking a knee during the national anthem and has been joined by other sports figures, published a video on Instagram on Wednesday that he described as "painful to watch."

It was of Zianna Oliphant, a 9-year-old girl from Charlotte, N.C., speaking at a City Council meeting on Monday after the fatal police shooting of Keith Lamont Scott.

"I feel like that we are treated differently than other people," she said, pausing tearfully.

"We are black people and we shouldn't have to feel like this. We shouldn't have to protest because you all are treating us wrong. We do this because we need to and have rights.

"I've been born and raised in Charlotte and I never felt this way until now," she said.

"It is a shame that our fathers and mothers are killed and we can't even see them anymore. It's a shame that we have to go to the graveyard and bury them. We have tears and shouldn't have tears."

Ms. Williams, who signed off her Facebook post with the words, "I Won't Be Silent," noted that her nephew was "so innocent," but so were "the others."

"I am a total believer that not 'everyone' is bad," she wrote. "It is just the ones that are ignorant, afraid, uneducated and insensitive that is affecting millions and millions of lives. Why did I have to think about this in 2016?"

Away From Main Stages, a Victorious Serena Williams Sees Inequality

BY CHRISTOPHER CLAREY | JUNE 23, 2011

WIMBLEDON, ENGLAND — She may be the defending champion and the potential comeback story of the year, but Serena Williams is touring the grounds again at the All England Club.

After triumphing on Centre Court in the first round, she was back in formation Thursday — security guards in front and behind — as she made her way through the dense crowds on the south side of Wimbledon to complete her appointed round at Court 2.

"They like to put us on Court 2, me and Venus, for whatever reason," Williams said after beating Simona Halep of Romania, 3-6, 6-2, 6-1. "I haven't figured it out yet. Maybe one day we'll figure it out."

Scheduling remains an issue at all the Grand Slam tournaments, but there has been a recurring debate at Wimbledon about gender equity. Larry Scott, the former chief of the Women's Tennis Association, publicly expressed concern to the All England Club in 2008 after the Williams sisters and Jelena Jankovic were not assigned to the two main courts for their fourth-round matches.

Scott, with support from his leading players, was able to change the club's mind on prize money, securing equal pay for the women in 2007. But tensions linger, and though Serena Williams has won four Wimbledon singles titles and Venus has won five, they have been asked to play on Court 2 this week while the four leading men — Roger Federer, Rafael Nadal, Novak Djokovic and Britain's Andy Murray — have played all of their matches on Centre Court or Court 1.

"They're never moved across," Williams said. "Actually, Venus and I have won more Wimbledons by ourselves than a lot of the players, or by ourselves in doubles even. So you know, at the end of the day, I don't know. Like I said, they're not going to change, doesn't look like."

Stacey Allaster, now head of the women's tour, supported Williams's comments.

"I share her disappointment," Allaster said in a statement. "Scheduling decisions at Wimbledon are made by the All England Club and only they would be able to explain the rationale behind their decision for the scheduling of Serena's match today."

The club, when asked for comment, released a statement: "Match scheduling at Wimbledon is a complex business and involves the referee and his experienced team in trying to achieve a fair and balanced draw from many competing interests and wishes, including the players. There is certainly no intention to favor any player or players."

Part of the problem is that Wimbledon generally schedules three singles matches on Centre Court and Court 1 while the French Open, where matches start earlier, schedules four per day on each of its two principal show courts. With three slots to fill, the club generally schedules two men's singles matches and one women's singles match on its two main courts. Friday's Court 1 schedule — perhaps in deference to this latest round of complaints — features two women's matches and one men's match.

The women's match that was put on Centre Court on Thursday was between Li Na of China and Sabine Lisicki of Germany, understandable in light of Li's victory in the French Open and the challenge posed by Lisicki, who pulled off the upset. The women's match scheduled on Court 1 was Maria Sharapova's versus Laura Robson, a 17-year-old who is Britain's best women's prospect. That match was not played because of rain delays.

If Williams had been scheduled (and postponed) on Court 1, she might have had to play singles matches on consecutive days, no simple task for a champion working her way back into top physical condition after missing nearly a year of competition because of health problems.

"I think Serena right now is playing about 49 or 50 percent, so I think it will be a while before she gets back to where she should be at," said Richard Williams, her father and coach.

Since returning from an 11-month break from the game last week in Eastbourne, she has been pushed to three sets in all four of her matches and struggled with her consistency from the baseline and her timing with returns. Her movement, particularly in transition, has also been below her best standard. But her overall level, after such an extended absence, has been remarkably high, and she has produced some brilliant play, brimming with her trademark power and has 58 winners and 37 unforced errors in two matches.

Convincing tennis was required for her to thwart Halep, an impressive server for her height (5 feet 6 inches) and an athletic, all-court talent who looked anything but intimidated by Williams and her 13 Grand Slam singles titles in the early going.

It should not get easier for Williams, who is seeded seventh based on her prior excellence. She will face her first seeded opponent — the Russian counterpuncher Maria Kirilenko, who is No. 26 — in the third round.

Serena Williams: Why Tennis Needs the Miami Open

ESSAY | BY SERENA WILLIAMS | MARCH 22, 2016

Editor's note: The Miami Open, a joint ATP/WTA tournament that began this week, is subject to a legal battle over possible renovations to the site, which is a public park. The dispute has led to speculation that the event, one of the biggest tennis tournaments in the United States, will move.

PEOPLE OFTEN SAY, "Home is where the heart is." As a professional tennis player, I've crisscrossed the world more than 20 times over, and along the way found a few places I've come to consider home. London, Melbourne, Paris, New York, Madrid and Rome are all cities I hold dear.

But one place that's been a true home for me over the past 20 years is Miami, the host of one of the world's most special sporting events: the Miami Open.

I grew up in Compton, Calif., and moved to West Palm Beach, Fla., at 9 years old. Every March, my dad would take Venus and me to Crandon Park on Key Biscayne for what was then called the Lipton International Players Championships. Miami is where I had the chance to watch some of the greats compete.

Little did I know back then, sitting on the sideline with braids in my hair, but I was about to embark on an incredible life journey that would see me play at the Miami Open across three decades.

When I think about the Miami Open having to leave a city I love because it isn't able to make improvements that would benefit the players and fans, it saddens me.

I made my first appearance there in 1998, reaching the quarterfinals. The next year, Venus and I faced off in the final, in what would be the first of our 11 finals meetings. I was coming off back-to-back tournament wins and riding high with confidence. But Venus has always been my most challenging opponent, the best player I've ever played.

It was an incredible day for our family, and I remember my nervous excitement before the match. My dad held a sign that read, "Welcome to the Williams Show." After I lost the first set, he switched it to another sign, "Go, Serena. Go!" A capacity crowd of 14,000 shouted from the stands, "Go, Williams!"

I think my dad was more nervous than Venus and me combined, but he was so proud of how far we'd come and what each of us had achieved. Venus beat me that day and went on to win the Miami Open in 1998, 1999 and 2001. I made sure we kept it in the family, following up with the first of my eight Miami Open wins in 2002.

The tournament's attendance through the years has continued to increase, and I've been fortunate to have the fans' loyal support. I hear "Come on, Serena!" cheers in many languages when I play in Miami. I love the diversity and the passion of the crowds. The mix of cultures and the incredible energy make it so fun to play.

The Miami Open has played an important role in my life and the lives of so many others. The event has always supported up-and-coming players, giving wild cards over the years to Pete Sampras, Andre Agassi, Andy Roddick, Steffi Graf, Monica Seles and James Blake before anyone had heard of them. In 1997, the tournament offered a wild card to Venus when she was just 16 years old.

Miami also helped lead the way for gender equality in the tennis world. Before 1985, the only combined men's and women's events were the four Grand Slams. In its inaugural year, the Miami Open broke that convention and featured both men and women.

Perhaps even more significant, the Miami Open paid equal prize money to men and women during the first staging of the event in 1985. In 2007, a decade after playing in her first Miami Open tournament, Venus led the successful battle for equal prize money for women at Wimbledon, ensuring that all four Grand Slam events paid women and men equally. The Miami Open had carried out Venus's vision of equality two decades earlier.

As a tennis tournament, Miami has always achieved greatly despite the odds. It doesn't take place in the biggest city; it's not the oldest, nor is it the most traditional. But the tournament keeps moving forward, finding creative ways of improving each year.

Leaving Miami would be a blow to our sport, to the city of Miami and to me. The tournament has, in many ways, set the standard for tennis events around the world in a unique time and place, and I hope we can all work together to improve this home court.

I am so grateful for the opportunities the Miami Open has afforded Venus and me, and I can't wait to get another chance at holding that trophy a week from Saturday.

SERENA WILLIAMS, a 21-time Grand Slam singles champion, is ranked No. 1 on the WTA Tour. She is represented by WME/IMG, which also owns the Miami Open.

Starring Serena Williams as Herself

BY CHRISTOPHER CLAREY | APRIL 27, 2018

ON A GRAY, GLOOMY Wednesday in Manhattan, Serena Williams was swaddled in bath towels to stay warm in an air-conditioned corner suite on the 41st floor of the Lotte New York Palace Hotel. The room's normally panoramic view had been obscured by dense fog, making it a challenge to see even across the street.

That seemed an apt metaphor for Williams's tennis career as she comes back from maternity leave at age 36.

It remains unclear whether she will be able to return to dominance. As she heads to Europe to start her clay-court season, she has played in only two tournaments in 2018, winning two matches and losing two and struggling, understandably, to regain full fitness.

But her personal life is a much clearer, blue sky matter. She is newly married to Alexis Ohanian, the internet entrepreneur and co-founder of Reddit, and is embracing the challenges of motherhood with their 8-month-old daughter, Olympia.

"We haven't been apart from each other more than 24 hours, ever," Williams said of her daughter, whom Williams's longtime fitness trainer, Mackie Shilstone, calls Baby O.

Williams's private sphere is about to become much more transparent with the premiere on Wednesday of a five-part series on HBO called "Being Serena," which tracks her pregnancy, her life-threatening postnatal problems and her comeback in remarkably unvarnished fashion.

The cameras follow her and Ohanian through some of the most intimate moments of their lives: even into the delivery room during Olympia's birth by cesarean section as Ohanian murmurs, "So proud of you," into his wife's ear. That is only moments before they get their first look at their new "teammate," Williams's splayed fingers mirroring Olympia's outstretched arms with a clear, plastic barrier still separating mother and child. Olympia is soon placed on Williams's chest and immediately stops crying.

The scene and the series are all the more surprising in light of Williams's longtime reluctance to share much publicly about her previous relationships, or even acknowledge them.

But she is in a new phase, and she reveals herself with few limits: letting the public see her concerns, her fears, her puffy eyes, her extra pounds, her surgical scar and her sense of humor, which is rarely in evidence when she's in her fist-clenching, turf-defending mode on the tennis court.

"A lot of people see me on the court, and they only judge and see that side of me, and there's so much more to my life and to me," she told me. "That's not me, actually to be honest, on the court. As much a part of my life as it is, I become a different person when I play tennis. The second I step onto the facilities, the grounds, I become a different person, and the second I step off, I'm back to being Serena, no pun intended.

"So I thought it would be interesting, while we were going through this process, if I just took all the curtains away, and I was just myself."

'I'M NO DIFFERENT THAN ANYONE ELSE'

Williams said she was the one who initiated the process with the HBO series.

"It was super-organic," she said. "When I found out I was pregnant, I was saying, 'I really want to get some footage of me,' because I remember my dad had all this film when we were younger, all this cool footage, and I wanted to start this journey for Olympia, even though she was the size of a raspberry at the time."

She shared the thought with her agent, Jill Smoller.

"HBO got wind of it, and they said, 'We would love to do it for you,'" Williams said. "My original idea was to do more just Olympia stuff, and then I thought if we're going to do this, let's go all out."

Mission accomplished, though some will certainly wonder whether some of this qualifies as oversharing in an era seemingly dedicated to it. But there are scenes of raw emotional power: above all, the moment when Williams has finally left the hospital after being treated for a pulmonary embolism and other blood-clotting issues in the harrowing days after delivery.

As she and Ohanian arrive at their house in Palm Beach Gardens, Fla., Williams emerges from the car, struggling to put one foot in front of the other as she lugs Olympia in a baby carrier with her right hand as if nothing — truly nothing — is going to stop her from reaching the front door.

"I didn't want to let her go; I don't want to let her go," Williams explained to me. "I like to believe, and I would like other people to understand, that I'm no different than anyone else. I have the same struggles a lot of women have had, and a lot of women are probably determined to carry their baby in the door. And a lot of women are determined to do a lot of the stuff that I do, and there's literally no difference between me and them with the exception of the side of me that just so happens to play professional tennis."

Her tennis success is, of course, what has brought her a global platform and considerable wealth, along with 23 Grand Slam singles trophies — the most recent of which was won at the 2017 Australian Open when she was two months pregnant with Olympia.

That trophy now sits on a small shelf in Olympia's room.

"It was definitely my idea because I feel like it's hers," Williams said. "It's sitting in her bedroom, and one day she will understand it, and I hope if we are fortunate enough to have more kids that they won't be jealous."

During the HBO series, when Ohanian repositions the trophy as the couple prepares for Olympia's birth, Williams chides him: "Lex, don't break it. You'll never have one."

After the delivery, as Williams lies in a hospital bed applying makeup and looking into a hand-held mirror, Ohanian asks, "What did you say when someone said that our little girl was going to win Wimbledon in like 15, 20 years?"

DAMON WINTER/THE NEW YORK TIMES

Serena Williams is trying to regain her dominant form after taking a maternity leave from the women's tour. She is also the subject of a five-part HBO series.

Williams, as if on cue, puts the mirror aside and answers, "Not if I'm still on tour!" to which a deeply amused Ohanian responds, "You're ridiculous."

There is much more of this banter, and at one stage, Williams expresses surprise that she and Ohanian "are such a good fit."

"I'm an athlete," she says. "He's a business guy. I'm black. He's white. We are totally opposite. I think we just complement each other. I think we understand hard work in different ways."

Anyone who has read Richard Williams's 2014 memoir, "Black and White: The Way I See It," knows how much resentment he felt about the racism he faced growing up in the American South and how intent he was on preparing his tennis-playing daughters to handle being outsiders in a predominantly white sport. Racist comments that he said he heard at the tournament in Indian Wells, Calif., in 2001 were a big part of the reason Serena and Venus Williams boycotted the event for more than a decade.

I asked Serena, who had dated black men and white men, what message her marriage to Ohanian sent.

"Oh my God," she said. "Literally all I tell Alexis is, 'well, you know, there's such a difference between white people and black people.' He always gets to hear about the injustices that happen; that wouldn't happen if I were white. It's interesting. I never thought I would have married a white guy, either, so it just goes to show you that love truly has no color, and it just really goes to show me the importance of what love is. And my dad absolutely loves Alexis."

She added: "Ultimately I wanted to be with someone who treated me nice, someone who was able to laugh with me and someone who understood my life and someone that loved me.

"And you know, I'm sure there's other people out there," she said, pausing for effect and then laughing. "But you know, Alexis is the one I connected with, and I wouldn't have it any other way."

In the series, as they finally settle into the front seat of their car to leave the hospital, she turns to Ohanian and says, a bit groggily, "I think we should have another baby," to which Ohanian responds — all too aware of what they went through in the previous days — "Can we at least get home with the first one?"

Williams told me she did not remember her comment until she saw the video. "I must have been crazy," she said, laughing. "I was clearly on something."

But she acknowledges, nearly eight months later, that the desire remains strong. "Oh yeah, if I wasn't wanting to play tennis," she said, "I definitely would have talked Alexis into having a baby already."

MORE REASONABLE EXPECTATIONS

Williams's comeback to tennis has not been without setbacks or indignities. She has needed more time than she expected to drop weight and go deep in tournaments. After her most recent match, an error-strewn first-round loss to Naomi Osaka at the Miami Open, Williams made the rare decision to skip the mandatory postmatch news conference, incurring a fine, and to head straight for her car with her bags to drive home.

"I played … obscenity," she said, pausing and managing to avoid the four-letter option.

"So I just thought after match point, I just thought there's no need," she added, referring to the news conference. "Such an easy shot, and I think I almost hit someone in the stands."

At the memory, Williams started to laugh uproariously, the sound reverberating through the suite. "And the best part was I passed Venus, and Venus looked at me and said, "I get it; oh, I get it,' " she said.

Venus also has declined to speak with the news media on some occasions after painful early-round losses, but Serena, like her big sister, is intent on using the setback for fuel.

"I feel like I set my expectations incredibly high, and I feel like after Miami, I wanted to get more, not realistic expectations, but more

DAMON WINTER/THE NEW YORK TIMES

Williams has expressed surprise that she and Ohanian are such a good fit. "We are totally opposite," she says. "I think we just complement each other."

LIFE IN THE SPOTLIGHT AND ADVOCACY **199**

reasonable expectations for me," Serena Williams said. "And so took some time off and then started training like a lot, lot, lot, lot, lot, lot, lot, lot, lot." Williams's eyes darted back and forth with each "lot" as if she were watching a long baseline rally. Shilstone, her trainer, said he told her after Miami: "Serena, you know how to play tennis. You are just not fit."

More than five weeks after the Osaka defeat, Shilstone said, Williams's fitness level is back up to "about 75 percent" of what it was when she won the 2017 Australian Open.

"Let me tell you, yesterday over at the hotel, we just did over 500 repetitions on the whole body with cords and cables," he said. "It was unbelievable, 500, and we did it in 45 minutes. Serena says: 'Mackie, now that I have a baby, I can't go two hours or whatever. We've got to get it done quick.' And I said, 'No, we've got to get it done smart.'"

Williams has a full-time nanny and is getting considerable childcare help from her mother, Oracene Price. But like many a working parent, Williams said she would like to clone herself, except that at this stage she would need "a clone army" because of her increasingly dense mix of business interests outside tennis.

She and Olympia will soon head to France, where Williams will train at her coach Patrick Mouratoglou's academy near Nice. She said she was not yet certain to play in the WTA Premier Mandatory event in Madrid, which begins on May 5, but is "definitely" playing in Rome the following week and at the French Open, which would be her first Grand Slam tournament since her comeback began.

"I feel like since Miami, I've made a ton of progress, but who knows," she said. "I'll have to see when I get out there to play a match. I always have to be ready, but I have to be even more ready because who knows who I can play early, or first or second. So I really have to be super-super-ready, so that's kind of what I've been working on."

Williams has a protected ranking of No. 1 that guarantees her entry into tournaments. But just like players returning from long-term injuries, she does not have a protected seeding that would help her avoid playing high-ranked players in early rounds. There has been a push within the WTA to reconsider that rule for players returning from pregnancy. Williams is in favor of protected seedings, arguing that women should not be discouraged from having families during their playing careers.

"I think it's more of a protection for women to have a life," Williams said. "You shouldn't have to wait to have a baby until you retire. If you want to have a baby and take a few months off or a year off and then come back, you shouldn't have to be penalized for that. Pregnancy is not an injury."

It certainly has cost Williams physically, though. She calls this comeback "the biggest challenge" of her career.

"I never felt winded like that," she said of her early practice sessions. "And it felt like no matter what I do, the weight is taking forever to get off, and it was crazy. Finally I was able to get better, but it took forever."

Ion Tiriac, the owner of the Madrid tournament, where Williams is likely to play next, referred to her weight when asked about Williams and the state of the women's game in a recent interview with Sport Bild, a German publication.

"With all due respect, 36 years old and 90 kilograms," or 198 pounds, Tiriac said, adding that he wished women's tennis had more headliners.

"I always say people are entitled to their opinion," said Williams, a two-time champion in Madrid, after being informed of the comment. "Clearly there's more to women's tennis than me. There's a lot more, but I'll have words with him, believe me, I'll have words with him. It's an ignorant comment, and it's a sexist comment, and maybe he's an ignorant man."

Asked why it had been so difficult to drop weight, Williams attributed it to her continuing to breast-feed. She had decided to stop earlier this month, but she was instructed by doctors to continue because she had developed mastitis, an infection of the breast tissue caused in her case by the plugging of the milk ducts. The infection contributed to her practicing little between her third-round loss to Venus Williams in Indian Wells and her match with Osaka in Miami.

"Apparently 10 percent of women get it," Serena Williams said. "So you have to continue to pump and feed until it clears. I'm finally ready to stop a little bit mentally, but it's definitely going to be hard."

Consider that yet another challenge for Williams, who has been through so many of them in her 23-year professional career and yet still claims to thrive on them. She maintains that next season, not this season, will be the right time to judge where her tennis truly is. Whenever the end of her career comes, she wants a big-bang finish.

"Eventually I'm going to have to drop that mic, and I would like for it to be a mic drop moment," she said.

Winning the 2017 Australian Open with Olympia along for the ride would, of course, have been an excellent one.

"It could have been the one," Williams said, the fog still obscuring the view of the Manhattan skyline. "But I'm still here, still playing."

The Meaning of Serena Williams

BY CLAUDIA RANKINE | AUG. 15, 2015

THERE IS NO MORE exuberant winner than Serena Williams. She leaps into the air, she laughs, she grins, she pumps her fist, she points her index finger to the sky, signaling she's No. 1. Her joy is palpable. It brings me to my feet, and I grin right back at her, as if I've won something, too. Perhaps I have.

There is a belief among some African-Americans that to defeat racism, they have to work harder, be smarter, be better. Only after they give 150 percent will white Americans recognize black excellence for what it is. But of course, once recognized, black excellence is then supposed to perform with good manners and forgiveness in the face of any racist slights or attacks. Black excellence is not supposed to be emotional as it pulls itself together to win after questionable calls. And in winning, it's not supposed to swagger, to leap and pump its fist, to state boldly, in the words of Kanye West, "That's what it is, black excellence, baby."

Imagine you have won 21 Grand Slam singles titles, with only four losses in your 25 appearances in the finals. Imagine that you've achieved two "Serena Slams" (four consecutive Slams in a row), the first more than 10 years ago and the second this year. A win at this year's U.S. Open would be your fifth and your first calendar-year Grand Slam — a feat last achieved by Steffi Graf in 1988, when you were just 6 years old. This win would also break your tie for the most U.S. Open titles in the Open era, surpassing the legendary Chris Evert, who herself has called you "a phenomenon that once every hundred years comes around." Imagine that you're the player John McEnroe recently described as "the greatest player, I think, that ever lived." Imagine that, despite all this, there were so many bad calls against you, you were given as one reason video replay needed to be used on the courts. Imagine that you have to contend with critiques of your body that perpetuate racist notions that black women are hypermasculine and unattractive. Imagine being asked to comment at a news conference before a tournament because the president of the Russian Tennis Federation, Shamil Tarpischev, has described you and your sister as "brothers" who are "scary" to look at. Imagine.

The word "win" finds its roots in both joy and grace. Serena's grace comes because she won't be forced into stillness; she won't accept those racist projections onto her body without speaking back; she won't go gently into the white light of victory. Her excellence doesn't mask the struggle it takes to achieve each win. For black people, there is an unspoken script that demands the humble absorption of racist assaults, no matter the scale, because whites need to believe that it's no big deal. But Serena refuses to keep to that script. Somehow, along the way, she made a decision to be excellent while still being Serena. She would feel what she feels in front of everyone, in response to anyone. At Wimbledon this year, for example, in a match against the home favorite Heather Watson, Serena, interrupted during play by the deafening support of Watson, wagged her index finger at the crowd and said, "Don't try me." She will tell an audience or an official that they are disrespectful or unjust, whether she says, simply, "No, no, no" or something much more forceful, as happened at the U.S. Open in 2009, when she told the lineswoman, "I swear to God I am [expletive] going to take this [expletive] ball and shove it down your [expletive] throat." And in doing so, we actually see her. She shows us her joy, her humor and, yes, her rage. She gives us the whole range of what it is to be human, and there are those who can't bear it, who can't tolerate the humanity of an ordinary extraordinary person.

In the essay "Everybody's Protest Novel," James Baldwin wrote, "our humanity is our burden, our life; we need not battle for it; we need only to do what is infinitely more difficult — that is, accept it." To accept the self, its humanity, is to discard the white racist gaze. Serena has freed herself from it. But that doesn't mean she won't be emotional or hurt by challenges to her humanity. It doesn't mean she won't battle for the right to be excellent. There is nothing wrong with Serena, but surely there is something wrong with the expectation that she be "good" while she is achieving greatness. Why should Serena not respond to racism? In whose world should it be answered with good manners? The notable difference between black excellence and white excellence is white excellence is achieved without having to battle racism. Imagine.

Two years ago, recovering from cancer and to celebrate my 50th birthday, I flew from LAX to J.F.K. during Serena's semifinal match at the U.S. Open with the hope of seeing her play in the final. I had just passed through a year when so much was out of my control, and Serena epitomized not so much winning as the pure drive to win. I couldn't quite shake the feeling (I still can't quite shake it) that my body's frailty, not the cancer but the depth of my exhaustion, had been brought on in part by the constant onslaught of racism, whether something as terrible as the killing of Trayvon Martin or something as mundane as the guy who let the door slam in my face. The daily grind of being rendered invisible, or being attacked, whether physically or verbally, for being visible, wears a body down. Serena's strength and focus in the face of the realities we shared oddly consoled me.

That Sunday in Arthur Ashe Stadium at the women's final, though the crowd generally seemed pro-Serena, the man seated next to me was cheering for the formidable tall blonde Victoria Azarenka. I asked him if he was American. "Yes," he said.

"We're at the U.S. Open. Why are you cheering for the player from Belarus?" I asked.

"Oh, I just want the match to be competitive," he said.

After Serena lost the second set, at the opening of the third, I turned to him again, and asked him, no doubt in my own frustration, why he was still cheering for Azarenka. He didn't answer, as was his prerogative. By the time it was clear that Serena was likely to win, his seat had been vacated. I had to admit to myself that in those moments I needed her to win, not just in the pure sense of a fan supporting her player, but to prove something that could never be proven, because if black excellence could cure us of anything, black people — or rather this black person — would be free from needing Serena to win.

"You don't understand me," Serena Williams said with a hint of impatience in her voice. "I'm just about winning." She and I were facing each other on a sofa in her West Palm Beach home this July. She looked at me with wariness as if to say, Not you, too. I wanted to talk about the tennis records that she is presently positioned either to tie or to break and had tried more than once to steer the conversation toward them. But she was clear: "It's not about getting 22 Grand Slams," she insisted. Before winning a calendar-year Grand Slam and matching Steffi Graf's record of 22 Slams, Serena would have to win seven matches and defend her U.S. Open title; those were the victories that she was thinking about.

She was wearing an enviable pink jumpsuit with palm trees stamped all over it as if to reflect the trees surrounding her estate. It was a badass outfit, one only someone of her height and figure could rock. She explained to me that she learned not to look ahead too much by looking ahead. As she approached 18 Grand Slam wins in 2014, she said, "I went too crazy. I felt I had to even up with Chris Evert and Martina Navratilova." Instead, she didn't make it past the fourth round at the Australian Open, the second at the French Open or the third at Wimbledon. She tried to change her tactics and focused on getting only to the quarterfinals of the U.S. Open. Make it to the second week and see what happens, she thought. "I started thinking like that, and then I got to 19. Actually I got to 21 just like that, so I'm not thinking about 22." She raised her water bottle to her lips, looking at me over its edge, as if to give me time to think of a different line of questioning.

Three years ago she partnered with the French tennis coach Patrick Mouratoglou, and I've wondered if his coaching has been an antidote to negotiating American racism, a dynamic that informed the coaching of her father, Richard Williams. He didn't want its presence to prevent her and Venus from winning. In his autobiography, "Black and White: The Way I See It," he describes toughening the girls' "skin" by bringing "busloads of kids from the local schools into Compton to surround the courts while Venus and Serena practiced. I had the kids call them every curse word in the English language, including 'Nigger,' " he writes. "I paid them to do it and told them to 'do their worst.' " His focus on racism meant that the sisters were engaged in two battles on and off the court. That level of vigilance, I know from my own life, can drain you. It's easier to shut up and pretend it's not happening, as the bitterness and stress build up.

Mouratoglou shifted Serena's focus to records (even if, as she prepares for a Slam, she says she can't allow herself to think about them). Perhaps it's not surprising that she broke her boycott against Indian Wells, where the audience notoriously booed her with racial epithets in 2001, during their partnership. Serena's decisions now seem directed toward building her legacy. Mouratoglou has insisted that she can get to 24 Grand Slams, which is the most won by a single player — Margaret Court — to date. Serena laughed as she recalled one of her earliest conversations with Mouratoglou. She told him: "I'm cool. I want to play tennis. I hate to lose. I want to win. But I don't have numbers in my head." He wouldn't allow that. "Now we are getting numbers in your head," he told her.

I asked how winning felt for her. I was imagining winning as a free space, one where the unconscious racist shenanigans of umpires, or the narratives about her body, her "unnatural" power, her perceived crassness no longer mattered. Unless racism destroyed the moment of winning so completely, as it did at Indian Wells, I thought it had to be the rare space free of all the stresses of black life. But Serena made it clear that she doesn't desire to dissociate from her history and her culture. She understands that even when she's focused only on winning, she is still representing. "I play for me," Serena told me, "but I also play and represent something much greater than me. I embrace that. I love that. I want that. So ultimately, when I am out there on the court, I am playing for me."

Her next possible victory is at the U.S. Open, the major where she has been involved in the most drama — everything from outrageous line calls to probations and fines. Serena admitted to losing her cool in the face of some of what has gone down there. In 2011, for example, a chair umpire, Eva Asderaki, ruled against Serena for yelling "Come on" before a point was completed, and as Serena described it to me, she "clutched her pearls" and told Asderaki not to look at her. But she said in recent years she finally felt embraced by the crowd. "No more incidents?" I asked. Before she could answer, we both laughed, because of course it's not wholly in her control. Then suddenly Serena stopped. "I don't want any incidents there," she said. "But I'm always going to be myself. If anything happens, I'm always going to be myself, true to myself."

I'm counting on it, I thought. Because just as important to me as her victories is her willingness to be an emotionally complete person while also being black. She wins, yes, but she also loses it. She jokes around, gets angry, is frustrated or joyous, and on and on. She is fearlessly on the side of Serena, in a culture that that has responded to living while black with death.

This July, the London School of Marketing (L.S.M.) released its list of the most marketable sports stars, which included only two women in its Top 20: Maria Sharapova and Serena Williams. They were ranked 12th and 20th. Despite decisively trailing Serena on the tennis court (Serena leads in their head-to-head matchups 18-2, and has 21 majors and 247 weeks at No. 1 to Sharapova's five majors and 21 weeks at number 1), Sharapova has a financial advantage off the court. This month Forbes listed her as the highest-paid female athlete, worth more than $29 million to Serena's $24 million.

When I asked Chris Evert about the L.S.M. list, she said, "I think the corporate world still loves the good-looking blond girls." It's a preference Evert benefited from in her own illustrious career. I suggested that this had to do with race. Serena, on occasion, has herself been a blonde. But of course, for millions of consumers, possibly not the right kind of blonde. "Maria was very aware of business and becoming a businesswoman at a much younger stage," Evert told me, adding, "She works hard." She also suggested that any demonstration of corporate preference is about a certain "type" of look or image, not whiteness in general. When I asked Evert what she made of Eugenie Bouchard, the tall, blond Canadian who has yet to really distinguish herself in the sport, being named the world's most marketable athlete by the British magazine SportsPro this spring, she said, with a laugh, "Well, there you have it." I took her statement to be perhaps a moment of agreement that Serena probably could not work her way to Sharapova's spot on Forbes's list.

"If they want to market someone who is white and blond, that's their choice," Serena told me when I asked her about her ranking. Her impatience had returned, but I wasn't sure if it was with me, the list or both. "I have a lot of partners who are very happy to work with me." JPMorgan Chase, Wilson Sporting Goods, Pepsi and Nike are among the partners she was referring to. "I can't sit here and say I should be higher on the list because I have won more." As for Sharapova, her nonrival rival, Serena was diplomatic: "I'm happy for her, because she worked hard, too. There is enough at the table for everyone."

There is another, perhaps more important, discussion to be had about what it means to be chosen by global corporations. It has to do with who is worthy, who is desirable, who is associated with the good life. As long as the white imagination markets itself by equating whiteness and blondness with aspirational living, stereotypes will remain fixed in place. Even though Serena is the best, even though she wins more Slams than anyone else, she is only superficially allowed to embody that in our culture, at least the marketable one.

But Serena was less interested in the ramifications involved in being chosen, since she had no power in this arena, and more interested in understanding her role in relation to those who came before her: "We have to be thankful, and we also have to be positive about it so the next black person can be No. 1 on that list," she told me. "Maybe it was not meant to be me. Maybe it's meant to be the next person to be amazing, and I'm just opening the door. Zina Garrison, Althea Gibson, Arthur Ashe and Venus opened so many doors for me. I'm just opening the next door for the next person."

I was moved by Serena's positioning herself in relation to other African-Americans. A crucial component of white privilege is the idea that your accomplishments can be, have been, achieved on your own. The private clubs that housed the tennis courts remained closed to minorities well into the second half of the 20th century. Serena reminded me that in addition to being a phenomenon, she has come out of a long line of African-Americans who battled for the right to be excellent in a such a space that attached its value to its whiteness and worked overtime to keep it segregated.

Serena's excellence comes with the ability to imagine herself achieving a new kind of history for all of us. As long as she remains healthy, she will most likely tie and eventually pass Graf's 22 majors, regardless of what happens at the U.S. Open this year. I want Serena to win, but I know better than to think her winning can end something she didn't start. But Serena is providing a new script, one in which winning doesn't carry the burden of curing racism, in which we win just to win — knowing that it is simply her excellence, baby.

CLAUDIA RANKINE is the author of five collections of poetry and the Aerol Arnold Professor of English at the University of Southern California. She last wrote for the magazine about mourning in the wake of the Charleston shootings. Her most recent work, "Citizen," was a finalist for the National Book Award and the winner of the National Book Critics Circle Award for poetry.

Glossary

aloof Possessing a cool and distant demeanor.

anticlimactic A disappointing end to an exciting set of events.

ballyhooed Extravagantly publicized.

baseline The line marking the end of the tennis court.

cathartic Causing the release of strong repressed emotions.

complacent Showing uncritical satisfaction with oneself.

conciliatory Peacemaking.

crescendo An increase in loudness or intensity.

erratic Unpredictable and out of control.

fraught Causing stress or anxiety.

hamper To impede in movement or progress.

iconoclastic Making an attack on cherished beliefs.

imposing Impressive in appearance.

infantilizing Treating someone like a child.

momentum The driving force of a moving body.

moxie Determination.

nadir The lowest point in one's life or career.

novice Someone inexperienced.

psyche The soul or mind.

unseeded Unranked relative to other players in a tournament.

Media Literacy Terms

"Media literacy" refers to the ability to access, understand, critically assess and create media. The following terms are important components of media literacy, and they will help you critically engage with the articles in this title.

angle The aspect of a news story that a journalist focuses on and develops.

attribution The method by which a source is identified or by which facts and information are assigned to the person who provided them.

balance Principle of journalism that both perspectives of an argument should be presented in a fair way.

bias A disposition of prejudice in favor of a certain idea, person, or perspective.

byline Name of the writer, usually placed between the headline and the story.

caption Identifying copy for a picture; also called a legend or cutline.

chronological order Method of writing a story presenting the details of the story in the order in which they occurred..

commentary Type of story that is an expression of opinion on recent events by a journalist, generally known as a commentator.

credibility The quality of being trustworthy and believable, said of a journalistic source.

editorial Article of opinion or interpretation.

feature story Article designed to entertain as well as to inform.

headline Type, usually 18 point or larger, used to introduce a story.

human interest story Type of story that focuses on individuals and how events or issues affect their life, generally offering a sense of relatability to the reader.

impartiality Principle of journalism that a story should not reflect a journalist's bias and should contain balance.

interview story A type of story in which the facts are gathered primarily by interviewing another person or persons.

motive The reason behind something, such as the publication of a news story or a source's perspective on an issue.

news story An article or style of expository writing that reports news, generally in a straightforward fashion and without editorial comment.

op-ed An opinion piece that reflects a prominent individual's opinion on a topic of interest.

paraphrase The summary of an individual's words, with attribution, rather than a direct quotation of their exact words.

quotation The use of an individual's exact words indicated by the use of quotation marks and proper attribution.

reliability The quality of being dependable and accurate, said of a journalistic source.

rhetorical device Technique in writing intending to persuade the reader or communicate a message from a certain perspective.

source The origin of the information reported in journalism.

sports reporting Type of story that reports on sporting events or topics related to sports.

tone A manner of expression in writing or speech.

Media Literacy Questions

1. Identify the various sources cited in the article "For Serena Williams, Childbirth Was a Harrowing Ordeal. She's Not Alone" (on page 177). How does Maya Salam attribute information to each of these sources in her article? How effective are Salam's attributions in helping the reader identify her sources?

2. In "After 'a Lot of Ups and Downs,' Serena Williams Nears Her Return" (on page 86), Christopher Clarey directly quotes Serena Williams and her coach, among others. What are the strengths of using a direct quote as opposed to a paraphrase? What are the weaknesses?

3. Compare the headlines of "Williamses' Rivalry Is Close and Compelling, if Not Classic" (on page 129) and "A Final Match for Venus and Serena Williams. But Maybe Not the Last One" (on page 133). Which is a more compelling headline, and why? How could the less compelling headline be changed to better draw the reader's interest?

4. What type of story is "Starring Serena Williams as Herself" (on page 194)? Can you identify another article in this collection that is the same type of story?

5. Does Selena Roberts demonstrate the journalistic principle of impartiality in her article "Williams Could Use an Etiquette Lesson" (on page 56)? If so, how did she do so? If not, what could she have included to make her article more impartial?

6. Does "A Family Tradition at Age 14" (on page 13) use multiple sources? What are the strengths of using multiple sources in a journalistic piece? What are the weaknesses of relying heavily on one source or a few sources?

7. What is the intention of the article "Tennis Needs Serena Williams Back. But Does She Need to Be Seeded?" (on page 90)? How effectively does it achieve its intended purpose?

8. Analyze the authors' perspectives in "Returning to the Top, but With a New View" (on page 65) and "Dominant in Her Era, Serena Still Has Time to Build on Legacy" (on page 73). Do you think one journalist is more impartial in their reporting than the other? If so, why do you think so?

9. Often, as a news story develops, a journalist's attitude toward a subject may change. Compare "Dominant in Her Era, Serena Still Has Time to Build on Legacy" (on page 73) and "Serena Williams Will Soon Be 35. But Will She Ever Be No. 1 Again?" (on page 77), both by Christopher Clarey. Did new information discovered between the publication of these two articles change Clarey's perspective?

10. The article "In This Sports Gender Gap, Men Fall Short." (on page 180) is an example of an op-ed. Identify how Will Leitch's attitude and tone help convey his opinion on the topic.

11. Identify each of the sources in " 'I Won't Be Silent': Serena Williams on the Fear of Driving While Black" (on page 184) as a primary source or a secondary source. Evaluate the reliability and credibility of each source. How does your evaluation of each source change your perspective on this article?

Citations

All citations in this list are formatted according to the Modern Language Association's (MLA) style guide.

BOOK CITATION

NEW YORK TIMES EDITORIAL STAFF, THE. *Serena Williams*. New York: New York Times Educational Publishing, 2019.

ONLINE ARTICLE CITATIONS

ARATON, HARVEY. "Sports of The Times; Center Stage for Families and Dramas." *The New York Times*, 4 July 2001, https://www.nytimes.com/2001/07/04/sports/sports-of-the-times-center-stage-for-families-and-dramas.html.

BELLAFANTE, GINIA. "Shopping With: Serena Williams; Game, Set, Dress Me In Leather." *The New York Times*, 18 Oct. 1999, https://www.nytimes.com/1999/10/17/style/shopping-with-serena-williams-game-set-dress-me-in-leather.html.

CLAREY, CHRISTOPHER. "After 'a Lot of Ups and Downs,' Serena Williams Nears Her Return." *The New York Times*, 9 Feb. 2018, https://www.nytimes.com/2018/02/09/sports/tennis/serena-williams-fed-cup.html.

CLAREY, CHRISTOPHER. "Another Sister Showdown for Williamses." *The New York Times*, 8 May 1998, https://www.nytimes.com/1998/05/08/sports/tennis-another-sister-showdown-for-williamses.html.

CLAREY, CHRISTOPHER. "Away From Main Stages, a Victorious Serena Williams Sees Inequality." *The New York Times*, 23 June 2011, https://www.nytimes.com/2008/07/05/sports/tennis/05williams.html.

CLAREY, CHRISTOPHER. "Dominant in Her Era, Serena Still Has Time to Build on Legacy." *The New York Times*, 10 Sept. 2012, https://www.nytimes.com/2012/09/11/sports/tennis/dominant-serena-williams-still-has-time-to-build-on-legacy.html.

CLAREY, CHRISTOPHER. "Failing to Find Rhythm, Serena Williams Ousted." *The New York Times*, 24 Jan. 2000, https://www.nytimes.com/2000/01/24/sports/tennis-failing-to-find-rhythm-serena-williams-ousted.html.

CLAREY, CHRISTOPHER. "A Final Match for Venus and Serena Williams. But Maybe Not the Last One." *The New York Times*, 26 Jan. 2017, https://www.nytimes.com/2017/01/26/sports/tennis/williams-venus-serena-australian-open.html.

CLAREY, CHRISTOPHER. "In Serena Williams's Comeback, a Familiar Opponent: Venus." *The New York Times*, 10 Mar. 2018, https://www.nytimes.com/2018/03/10/sports/in-serena-williamss-come-back-a-familiar-opponent-venus.html.

CLAREY, CHRISTOPHER. "On the Doubles Court, Venus and Serena Williams Make Time Stand Still." *The New York Times*, 1 June 2018, https://www.nytimes.com/2018/06/01/sports/serena-venus-williams-french-open.html.

CLAREY, CHRISTOPHER. "The 'Real Serena' Emerges and Roars Back at the French Open." *The New York Times*, 31 May 2018, https://www.nytimes.com/2018/05/31/sports/serena-williams-french-open.html.

CLAREY, CHRISTOPHER. "Serena Williams and Maria Sharapova to Reboot a Rivalry After Life Intervened." *The New York Times*, 2 June 2018, https://www.nytimes.com/2018/06/02/sports/french-open-serena-williams-maria-sharapova-.html.

CLAREY, CHRISTOPHER. "Serena Williams Isn't Able to Defend Her Title." *The New York Times*, 22 Jan. 2008, https://www.nytimes.com/2008/01/22/sports/tennis/22tennis.html.

CLAREY, CHRISTOPHER. "Serena Williams Will Soon Be 35. But Will She Ever Be No. 1 Again?" *The New York Times*, 9 Sept. 2016, https://www.nytimes.com/2016/09/10/sports/tennis/serena-williamss-young-rivals-are-posing-questions-she-cant-answer.html.

CLAREY, CHRISTOPHER. "Starring Serena Williams as Herself." *The New York Times*, 27 Apr. 2018, https://www.nytimes.com/2018/04/27/sports/tennis/serena-williams.html.

CLAREY, CHRISTOPHER. "Surprising Even Herself, Williams Rallies to Title." *The New York Times*, 9 Sept. 2012, https://www.nytimes.com/2012/09/10/sports/tennis/serena-williams-rallies-to-capture-us-open-title.html.

CLAREY, CHRISTOPHER. "Tennis Needs Serena Williams Back. But Does She Need to Be Seeded?" *The New York Times*, 28 May 2018, https://www.nytimes.com/2018/05/28/sports/tennis/serena-williams-french-open.html.

CLAREY, CHRISTOPHER. "Williamses' Rivalry Is Close and Compelling, if Not Classic." *The New York Times*, 5 July 2008, https://www.nytimes.com/2008/07/05/sports/tennis/05williams.html.

FINN, ROBIN. "A Family Tradition at Age 14." *The New York Times*, 31 Oct. 1995, https://www.nytimes.com/1995/10/31/sports/tennis-a-family-tradition-at-age-14.html.

FINN, ROBIN. "By Knocking Spirlea Out, Serena Williams May Get to Face Her Sister Next." *The New York Times*, 19 Jan. 1998, https://www.nytimes.com/1998/01/19/sports/tennis-by-knocking-spirlea-out-serena-williams-may-get-to-face-her-sister-next.html.

FINN, ROBIN. "In Williams vs. Williams, Big Sister Moves Ahead." *The New York Times*, 21 Jan. 1998, https://www.nytimes.com/1998/01/21/sports/tennis-in-williams-vs-williams-big-sister-moves-ahead.html.

FINN, ROBIN. "It's 3 Sets and Pout for Serena Williams." *The New York Times*, 29 May 1999, https://www.nytimes.com/1999/05/29/sports/tennis-it-s-3-sets-and-pout-for-serena-williams.html.

FINN, ROBIN. "Playing in Draw's Opposite Sides Benefits the Williamses and the Game." *The New York Times*, 21 Mar. 1999, https://www.nytimes.com/1999/03/21/sports/tennis-playing-in-draw-s-opposite-sides-benefits-the-williamses-and-the-game.html.

FINN, ROBIN. "Serena Williams Leaves Her Mark on Davenport." *The New York Times*, 8 Mar. 1999, https://www.nytimes.com/1999/03/08/sports/tennis-serena-willliams-leaves-her-mark-on-davenport.html.

FINN, ROBIN. "Serena Williams Will Put Streak on Line Against Hingis." *The New York Times*, 25 Mar. 1999, https://www.nytimes.com/1999/03/25/sports/tennis-serena-williams-will-put-streak-on-line-against-hingis.html.

FINN, ROBIN. "Teen-Ager, Fighting to Turn Pro at 14, Puts Off Lawsuit for Now." *The New York Times*, 6 Oct. 1995, https://www.nytimes.com/1995/10/06/sports/tennis-teen-ager-fighting-to-turn-pro-at-14-puts-off-lawsuit-for-now.html.

FINN, ROBIN. "U.S. Open; Little Sister Becomes the Stardust Half." *The New York Times*, 12 Sept. 1999, https://www.nytimes.com/1999/09/12/sports/us-open-little-sister-becomes-the-stardust-half.html.

FINN, ROBIN. "U.S. Open; Serena Williams Sizes Up Seles, and Wins." *The New York Times*, 9 Sept. 1999, https://www.nytimes.com/1999/09/09/sports/us-open-serena-williams-sizes-up-seles-and-wins.html.

FINN, ROBIN. "U.S. Open; Unstoppable Team Williams Takes Doubles Title." *The New York Times*, 13 Sept. 1999, https://www.nytimes.com/1999/09/13/sports/us-open-unstoppable-team-williams-takes-doubles-title.html.

HAUSER, CHRISTINE. " 'I Won't Be Silent': Serena Williams on the Fear of Driving While Black." *The New York Times*, 28 Sept. 2016, https://www.nytimes.com/2016/09/29/sports/tennis/serena-williams-addresses-fears-of-driving-while-black.html.

LEITCH, WILL. "In This Sports Gender Gap, Men Fall Short." *The New York Times*, 15 Sept. 2017, https://www.nytimes.com/2017/09/15/opinion/sports-gender-gap-serena.html.

MATHER, VICTOR, AND NAILA-JEAN MEYERS. "Grand Sibling Rivalry Leaves Venus Williams a Distinct Underdog." *The New York Times*, 27 Jan. 2017, https://www.nytimes.com/2017/01/27/sports/tennis/serena-venus-williams-australian-open.html.

MEYERS, NAILA-JEAN. "Serena Williams Wins Wimbledon, Tying Record for Grand Slam Singles Titles." *The New York Times*, 9 July 2016, https://www.nytimes.com/2016/07/10/sports/tennis/serena-williams-wins-wimbledon-beats-angelique-kerber.html.

RABIN, RONI CARYN. "Winning While Pregnant: How Athletes Do It." *The New York Times*, 27 Apr. 2017, https://www.nytimes.com/2017/04/27/well/move/winning-while-pregnant-how-athletes-do-it.html.

RANKINE, CLAUDIA. "The Meaning of Serena." *The New York Times*, 25 Aug. 2015, https://www.nytimes.com/2015/08/30/magazine/the-meaning-of-serena-williams.html.

ROBBINS, LIZ. "Noticed; Williamsmania Sweeps The Black A-List." *The New York Times*, 9 Sept. 2001, https://www.nytimes.com/2001/09/09/style/noticed-williamsmania-sweeps-the-black-a-list.html.

ROBBINS, LIZ. "The Tennis Balls Were White Once, Too." *The New York Times*, 3 Sept. 2000, https://www.nytimes.com/2000/09/03/weekinreview/ideas-trends-courts-of-public-opinion-the-tennis-balls-were-white-once-too.html.

ROBERTS, SELENA. "Serena Williams Needs Some of Agassi's Grit." *The New York Times*, 30 Aug. 2006, https://www.nytimes.com/2006/08/30/sports/tennis/30roberts.html.

ROBERTS, SELENA. "Serena Williams Wins As the Boos Pour Down." *The New York Times*, 18 Mar. 2001, https://www.nytimes.com/2001/03/18/sports/tennis-serena-williams-wins-as-the-boos-pour-down.html.

ROBERTS, SELENA. "Sydney 2000: Tennis; Who Could Ask for Anything More?"

The New York Times, 29 Sept. 2000, https://www.nytimes.com/2000/09/29/sports/sydney-2000-tennis-who-could-ask-for-anything-more.html.

ROBERTS, SELENA. "They're Young. They're Sexy. They're Targets." *The New York Times,* 1 July 2002, https://www.nytimes.com/2002/07/01/sports/tennis-they-re-young-they-re-sexy-they-re-targets.html.

ROBERTS, SELENA. "U. S. Open; Serena Williams Wins Match, Then Takes a Shot at Hingis." *The New York Times*, 3 Sept. 1999, https://www.nytimes.com/1999/09/03/sports/u-s-open-serena-williams-wins-match-then-takes-a-shot-at-hingis.html.

ROBERTS, SELENA. "Williams Could Use an Etiquette Lesson." *The New York Times*, 5 Sept. 2007, https://www.nytimes.com/2007/09/05/sports/tennis/05roberts.html.

ROBERTS, SELENA. "Williams Sisters Learned to Think Off Court, Too" *The New York Times*, 3 July 2000, https://www.nytimes.com/2000/07/03/sports/on-tennis-williams-sisters-learned-to-think-off-court-too.html.

ROBERTS, SELENA. "Williamses Aren't Outsiders, But They're Still Different." *The New York Times*, 25 Aug. 2002, https://www.nytimes.com/2002/08/25/sports/tennis-williamses-aren-t-outsiders-but-they-re-still-different.html.

ROBERTS, SELENA. "The Williamses, Reluctant Rivals, Will Battle for the French Title." *The New York Times*, 8 June 2002, https://www.nytimes.com/2002/06/08/sports/tennis-the-williamses-reluctant-rivals-will-battle-for-the-french-title.html.

ROTHENBERG, BEN. "For Serena Williams, a Memorable U.S. Open Final for the Wrong Reasons." *The New York Times*, 9 Sept. 2018, https://www.nytimes.com/2018/09/09/sports/tennis/serena-williams-sexism-us-open-.html.

ROTHENBERG, BEN. "Returning to the Top, but With a New View." *The New York Times*, 26 Oct. 2016, https://www.nytimes.com/2012/10/27/sports/tennis/serena-williams-back-on-the-rise-with-newfound-appreciation.html.

SAFRONOVA, VALERIYA. "Her U.S. Open Loss Behind Her, Serena Williams Turns to Fashion." *The New York Times*, 13 Sept. 2016, https://www.nytimes.com/2016/09/13/fashion/serena-williams-hsn-new-york-fashion-week.html.

SALAM, MAYA. "For Serena Williams, Childbirth Was a Harrowing Ordeal. She's Not Alone." *The New York Times*, 11 Jan. 2018, https://www.nytimes.com/2018/01/11/sports/tennis/serena-williams-baby-vogue.html.

STEVENS, MATT. "Serena Williams Gives Birth to a Baby Girl." *The New York Times*, 1 Sept. 2017, https://www.nytimes.com/2017/09/01/sports/serena-birth-baby.html.

THOMAS, KATIE. "Making Tennis the Top Priority Brings Serena Williams the No. 1 Ranking." *The New York Times*, 8 Sept. 2008, https://www.nytimes.com/2008/09/09/sports/tennis/09serena.html.

WILLIAMS, SERENA. "Serena Williams: Why Tennis Needs the Miami Open." *The New York Times*, 22 Mar. 2016, https://www.nytimes.com/2016/03/23/sports/tennis/serena-williams-miami-open.html.

ZANCA, SAL A. "Continents Apart, Williams Sisters Make History." *The New York Times*, 1 Mar. 1999, https://www.nytimes.com/1999/03/01/sports/tennis-continents-apart-williams-sisters-make-history.html.

Index

A

Agassi, Andre, 27, 29, 35, 41, 46, 53, 54–55, 157, 166, 168, 192
age restrictions, 11–12, 13, 90
Ashe, Arthur, 157, 159
  Stadium, 33, 56, 68, 77, 135, 150, 158, 205
Australian Open, 8, 9, 12, 17, 20, 21, 33, 39–40, 56–58, 59–62, 65, 68, 71, 74, 77, 82, 83, 86, 89, 96, 102, 103, 104, 106, 108, 111, 112, 114, 129, 130, 133–137, 138, 140–141, 142, 143, 144, 153, 175, 196, 200, 202, 206
Azarenka, Victoria, 69, 70, 71–72, 73, 90, 91, 93–94, 205

B

Barty, Ash, 95, 96, 149
"Being Serena," 194–197, 198
Bertens, Kiki, 101, 143, 145

C

Capriati, Jennifer, 11, 13, 15, 49–51, 126, 127, 128, 154, 163, 164, 166, 167
Clijsters, Kim, 11, 45–46, 47–48, 70, 73, 90, 93, 141, 144, 154, 159, 163, 168, 180
Coetzer, Amanda, 22, 113

Cornet, Alizé, 104, 153
Court, Margaret, 75, 89, 96, 103, 207

D

Davenport, Lindsay, 20–21, 28, 31, 32–34, 35, 40, 43, 50, 73, 93, 109, 147, 163, 180
Dementieva, Elena, 43, 130, 144
Djokovic, Novak, 61, 98, 104, 181, 182, 188
Dokic, Jelena, 123, 164, 167
doubles, 8, 21, 29, 35, 36, 42, 43, 44, 50, 60, 65, 69, 86–87, 108, 111, 119, 120–121, 129, 146, 147–149, 188

E

Evert, Chris, 35, 75, 97, 130, 157, 203, 206, 208–209

F

fashion in tennis, 155–157
Fed Cup, 75, 86–87, 89, 97, 121, 146
Federer, Roger, 61–62, 74, 181, 188
Fernandez, Mary Joe, 25–26
French Open, 8, 25–26, 37, 57, 66, 69, 76, 77, 88, 90, 92, 93, 95–98, 99–102, 126–128, 139, 147–149, 189, 200, 206
Fusai, Alexandra, 111, 112

G

Garrison, Zina, 43, 44, 210
gender inequality in tennis, 12, 188–190, 192
Gibson, Althea, 36, 210
Giorgi, Camila, 100–101
Görges, Julia, 95–96, 97–98, 99, 102, 148
Graf, Steffi, 37, 55, 75, 77, 105, 119, 134, 192, 203, 206, 210
Grand Slam, 8, 9, 11, 18, 31–32, 33, 35, 36–37, 39, 49, 60, 61, 65, 66, 68, 69, 70, 71, 73–75, 77, 79, 82, 87, 90, 92, 96, 98, 99, 103, 106, 109, 118, 120, 121, 130, 131, 133, 134, 135, 137, 138, 141, 142, 145, 148, 150, 155, 188, 190, 192, 196, 203, 206, 207

H

Halep, Simona, 78–79, 80, 91, 100, 101, 149, 188, 190
Henin, Justine, 11, 56–58, 59, 64, 73, 141, 167
Hingis, Martina, 11, 20, 22–23, 26, 28, 29–30, 35, 36–38, 40, 42, 46, 73, 108, 114, 120, 147, 162, 163, 166, 170
HSN (Home Shopping

Network), 173–174

I

Indian Wells, 22, 36, 45, 89, 118–119, 143–146, 167, 168, 197, 202, 207

J

Jankovic, Jelena, 59–60, 188
Jehovah's Witness, 8

K

Kerber, Angelique, 77, 101, 103–104, 105–107, 134
King, Billie Jean, 43, 44, 69–70, 75, 151, 156, 164
Kournikova, Anna, 14–15, 23, 147, 156, 161

L

Likhovtseva, Yelena, 39, 40
Lipton Championships, 21, 22, 23, 36, 117, 119, 191

M

Martinez, Conchita, 111, 112
Mauresmo, Amelie, 21, 73, 113, 114–115, 167
McEnroe, John, 44, 153, 181, 203
men's tennis, 23–24, 26–27, 28–29, 35, 41, 42, 46, 53, 54–55, 60–61, 104, 138, 152, 153, 157, 188
Miami Open, 90, 96, 145, 191–193, 199–200, 202
Miller, Anne, 14–15
Minella, Mandy, 92
Mouratoglou, Patrick, 66–67, 69, 75–76, 78, 80, 88, 89, 96, 152, 176, 200, 206, 207
Muguruza, Garbiñe, 77, 101

N

Nadal, Rafael, 104, 152, 188
Navratilova, Martina, 75, 119, 130, 167, 206
Nike, 10, 157, 162, 166, 209

O

Ohanian, Alexis (husband), 10, 83, 87, 102, 134, 175, 194, 196–197, 198
Ohanian, Olympia (daughter), 10, 87, 88, 96, 99, 104, 148, 175–176, 180, 194–195, 196, 200, 202
Olympics, 84, 174
  gold medals, 8, 42, 44, 65, 69, 73, 75
  London 2012, 65, 69, 70, 73, 75
  Rio de Janeiro 2016, 77, 78, 79, 80
  Sydney 2000, 42–44
  Tokyo 2020, 89
Osaka, Naomi, 96, 150–151, 199, 200, 202

P

Petkovic, Andrea, 100, 149
Pierce, Mary, 32, 33–34, 36, 39–40, 65, 109, 121, 147, 157
Pliskova, Karolina, 77, 79, 80–81, 96, 99, 102, 173
Pliskova, Kristyna, 90, 92
pregnancy and athletes, 82–85, 91–93
Price, Oracene "Brandy" Williams (mother), 15, 17–18, 52–53, 54, 55, 57, 60, 109, 111, 114, 118, 122, 124, 126, 127, 128, 129, 131, 170, 174, 200
Puma, 10, 118, 166, 171

R

race and racism, 123–124, 155, 167, 179, 184–187, 197–198, 203, 204–205, 206, 207, 208–210
Ramos, Carlos, 152–153
Razzano, Virginie, 69, 147
Reebok, 11, 118, 166
Rinaldi, Kathy, 87, 88
Roddick, Andy, 73, 192

S

Sampras, Pete, 24, 26, 28, 41, 46, 53, 138, 157, 192
Sanchez Vicario, Arantxa, 13, 19, 26, 110
Schett, Barbara, 23, 36, 121
Seles, Monica, 28, 32, 40, 42, 109, 112, 156, 161, 192
Sharapova, Maria, 59, 63, 72, 96, 99–102, 189, 208–209
Smoller, Jill, 77, 195
Spirlea, Irina, 17, 18, 109
Stephens, Sloane, 100–101, 180

T

Testud, Sandrine, 28, 40, 112, 120

U

U.S. Open, 8, 28–30, 31–34, 35–38, 40, 53, 63–64, 65, 68–72, 73–74, 77, 78–81, 93, 105, 109, 113, 118, 120–121, 124, 127, 130, 131, 135, 138, 140, 145, 148–149, 150–154, 155, 156, 157, 159, 165, 170, 173, 175, 180, 181, 203, 204, 205–206, 208, 210

V

Vandeweghe, Coco, 86, 87,

INDEX **223**

88, 98, 134, 137

W

Willams, Richard (father), 8, 12, 14, 15-16, 17, 21, 29-30, 36, 38, 45, 48, 50-51, 74, 109, 114, 116, 117, 119, 121, 122, 123, 124-125, 131, 144, 147, 159, 168, 189, 197, 206-207

Williams, Serena
  childhood, 8
  criticism of/controversy, 25-26, 45-48, 52, 53-54, 56-58, 64, 74, 90, 95, 124, 138, 150-154, 156, 167-168, 208
  doubles matches with Venus, 35-36, 42-44, 60, 108, 111, 119, 120-121, 129, 146, 147-149
  early career, 8, 11-51
  education, 8, 12
  fashion/clothing, 10, 29, 63, 66, 155-157, 158, 161, 170-172, 173-174
  HBO series, 194-197, 198
  injuries, 52, 53, 64, 78, 79-80, 93, 110
  issues important to, 10, 155, 184-187, 188-190, 191-193
  marriage, 10, 83, 87, 102, 134, 175, 194, 196-197, 198
  mid-career, 52-67
  popularity and fame of, 158-160, 161, 162, 163, 165-169, 196
  pregnancy and childbirth, 9-10, 68, 82-85, 86, 87, 90, 91, 93, 95, 96, 99, 101, 103, 104, 143, 148, 149, 150, 175-176, 177-179, 180, 181, 182-183, 194-195, 196, 201
  professional maturity, 68-107
  religion, 8, 45
  rivalry with and matches against Venus, 17-19, 22, 36, 64, 74, 86, 108-154, 163, 167-168, 191-192, 202
  stalker of, 162
  start in tennis, 8, 15
  ups and downs in career, 9, 52-54, 73, 78-79, 86-89, 90, 96-97, 198-201
  what she represents, 203-210

Williams, Venus, 8, 11, 16, 20, 21, 29, 35, 39, 45, 51, 62, 93, 191, 199, 210
  at Australian Open, 17-19, 57
  doubles matches with Serena, 35-36, 42-44, 60, 108, 111, 119, 120-121, 129, 146, 147-149
  early career, 11, 13, 14, 15, 40
  at Fed Cup, 86-87
  at French Open, 25
  at Lipton Championships, 22, 23
  popularity and fame of, 158-160, 161, 163, 165-169
  rivalry with and matches against Serena, 17-19, 22, 36, 64, 74, 86, 108-154, 163, 167-168, 191-192, 202
  at U.S. Open, 31, 64, 80, 120-121, 159, 165, 175

Wimbledon, 8, 9, 32, 35, 37, 49, 57, 63, 65, 68, 69, 70, 73, 74, 77, 78, 80, 88, 92, 93, 101-102, 103-107, 112, 113, 122-124, 129-132, 135, 137, 138, 140, 141-142, 148, 156, 159, 162, 167, 168, 174, 180, 188-190, 196, 204, 206

Witt, David, 131, 135-136

women in sports, private lives of, 180-183

Women's Tennis Association, 8, 11, 13, 50, 65, 77, 90-91, 93, 113, 114, 151, 161, 163, 188

Williams's threatened lawsuit against, 11-12, 14

women tennis players, fame and marketing of, 161-164, 208-209

Wozniacki, Caroline, 77, 174

This book is current up until the time of printing. For the most up-to-date reporting, visit www.nytimes.com.